"If there were Druids whose temples were

the oak groves, my temple is the swamp."

—Henry David Thoreau, *Journal*, January 4, 1853

Bland Simpson

The *Great* *Dismal*

A Swamp Memoir

Henry Holt and Company   New York

Henry Holt and Company, Inc.
Publishers since 1866
115 West 18th Street
New York, New York 10011

Henry Holt® is a registered trademark
of Henry Holt and Company, Inc.

Library of Congress Cataloging-in-Publication Data
Simpson, Bland.
    The Great Dismal : a swamp memoir / Bland Simpson.—
1st Owl book ed.
        p.   cm.
    Originally published: Chapel Hill : University of North Carolina
Press, c1990.
    Includes bibliographical references and index.
    1. Dismal Swamp (N.C. and Va.)—Description and travel.
2. Natural history—Dismal Swamp (N.C. and Va.)   3. Dismal Swamp
(N.C. and Va.)—Social life and customs.   4. Simpson, Bland—
Childhood and youth.   I. Title.
[F262.D7S56   1993]
975.5′523—dc20   93-12161
                                                            CIP

ISBN 0-8050-2535-9

First published in hardcover by The University of North Carolina
Press in 1990.

First Owl Book Edition—1993

Designed by April Leidig-Higgins

Printed in the United States of America
All first editions are printed on acid-free paper.∞

10   9   8   7   6   5   4   3   2   1

Visitors to the Great Dismal Swamp may write:
Great Dismal Swamp National Wildlife Refuge
Box 349
Suffolk, Virginia 23434

To Ann Cary Simpson
and Jerry Leath Mills

Contents

Acknowledgments

The wilderness that lay between the first two English settlements in America, Roanoke Island and Jamestown, has had our attention from the beginning, and held it. Through William Byrd II and scores of Swamp authors since, I have enjoyed many a journey into the Great Dismal, and have had the best of fellow travelers. I have also had a grand inspiration in the prose and person of Brooke Meanley, a man who with his wife Anna has found here in this Swamp the strength and marrow of nature, and to them and these others whose help and encouragement have seen me through the Swamp goes my deepest gratitude: Olive Camp Johnson, H. G. Jones and the wonderful staff of the North Carolina Collection in Chapel Hill, Tom and Page Massengale, David Perry, Surry Parker Roberts, and two stalwarts— my old friend Jake, and my dear wife Ann. To all those who speak through these pages I offer my thanks, to all the living and the dead.

 *The Great Dismal*

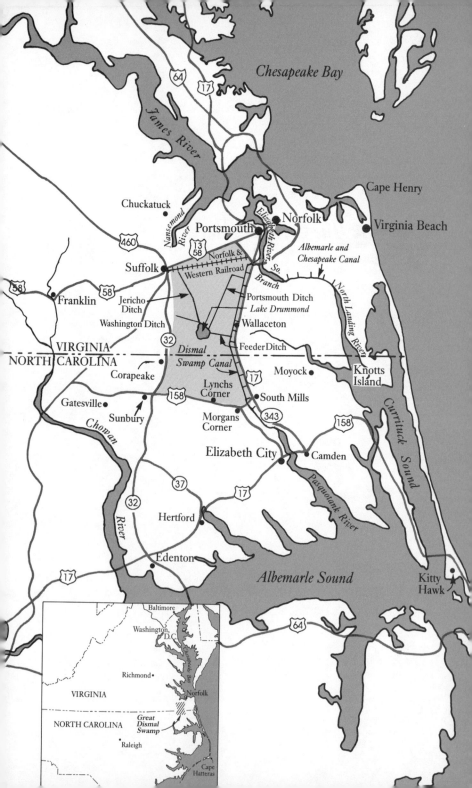

1

Drummond's Pond

"One thinks if God ever made a fairer sheet of water, it
is yet hidden away from the eyes of mortals."
—Alexander Hunter, *A Huntsman in the South*, 1908

When I was a boy, my father and I used to go out
boating on the broad, black Pasquotank River, running through Elizabeth City, North Carolina. We
had a 1¼ horsepower motor that stayed clamped to a sawhorse in
our garage until the Saturday or Sunday afternoons when he would
haul it forth and put it in the trunk of our maroon humpback '52
Dodge and we would drive to a boathouse on the Camden causeway
across the Pasquotank, rent a gray wooden skiff, and set out from
there.

Ours was a riverine world, and the dark water was everywhere.
Already on our ride to the causeway we would have crossed Gaith-
er's Lagoon, where my first boating had been in an unseaworthy
forty-gallon washbucket, then gone for a mile along Riverside Drive
on the western shore, past houses on stilts out over the water and
past the millionaire oilman's yacht and the machineshops and marine railways and the yacht club that put on the hydroplane races
each fall, then up and over dark Charles Creek and right at Dog
Corner, along Water Street past the fishhouse and onto the big
drawbridge itself.

Here a ferry once led to the Floating Road to Camden, before the
bridge and causeway, but I didn't know that then. I had no notion
that anything had ever been different than it was now, or ever would
be. In our little gray skiff my father would guide us unhurriedly past
the short cypress trees in the shallows. He had been a pilot and a
navigator in the Navy during World War II, and when we were well
out he would give me the motor handle, pick a heading, and in a

bemused nautical fashion say something like, "Steer her for that stob yonder, sailor!"

Legions of turtles basked on logs and timbers at the river's edge, and we saw water moccasins and muskrats gliding in the shadows of treelimbs hanging way out from shore. Always we went upstream—for the river became too broad a bay below town for us to venture south—around the horseshoe curve where the Pasquotank narrowed, past the burned-out shell of the Dare Lumber Company and the rotting pilings of the long-gone oyster-shucking houses, then under the tawny drawbridge, where the momentary dark and the echoed drone of the little engine as we passed beneath always thrilled me.

Alongside old wharves where steamboats once called we would cruise lazily for a bit, never going any farther upriver than a point even with a great grain elevator, about a mile from where we had begun. I could see how the river was narrowing still, and I wondered: where did it go from here? If someday we kept on, instead of turning downstream for the boathouse and home, where would it take us?

If we followed it all the way, my father used to tell me, we would disappear with the river into the Great Dismal Swamp.

≈

We would not have been the first.

The Great Dismal has been around for ten thousand years, five hundred generations, and some unknown Indian man, woman, or child who sleeps deep beneath the mantle of peat, the floor of this great boggy wood, unremarked and unmourned holds that honor. The Powhatan had hunted the Swamp in that ancient age when it was a great reach of open marsh. Their bola-weights, spheres and ovoids and dimpled stones once thonged together and slung at waterfowl, have turned up all over the vast morass, most along the Suffolk Scarp, the ancient Pleistocene seabeach at the Swamp's western edge. So have their projectile points, the tools and weapons they went to once the broad marsh had grown up in boreal forest, jack pines and spruce.

The Ice Age had ended and the climate warmed, and the cold-weather woods fell in succession to new forests, first of beech and birch, then of oak and hickory, and these went down in turn to a wet stretch of cypress and gum and a cedar here called juniper. Still the Powhatan were in the Great Dismal, and not just to hunt. They left behind them potsherds and pollen, the spore of maize, grains too heavy to be wind-borne far from where they grew—the Indians were farming at the very heart of the Swamp.

Nansemond was the name of one of thirty peoples that Wahunsonacock—Chief Powhatan, father of Pocahontas—counted among his empire in the early 1600s. Their home then was in the Swamp along the Suffolk Scarp, but three centuries after Jamestown a few of them clustered together around the village of Chuckatuck, north of Suffolk, Virginia, in the 1930s, there to die out as timber outfits great and small cut the last of the Swamp's virgin forest. None now speak that tongue, but in my lifetime a Nansemond named Earl Bass hunted the Swamp from the north side.

From car windows as a boy I stared at Earl Bass's Swamp, the corridor of switch cane and big pines between Suffolk and Norfolk that is U.S. 13/58. And I saw the cypress go to gold and rust each autumn in the sloughs along U.S. 158, between Morgans Corner and Sunbury. My Ferebee cousins in Camden carried me into the Swamp's southern edge, for it was their own backyard, and we its diminutive natives. I was no Nansemond, but I knew I was Powhatan aplenty from the moment my great-aunt Jennie told me I was kin to Pocahontas—that through the Virginia Blands a smidgen of her blood ran in my veins.

Mostly I knew the Swamp from countless rides up and down the Canalbank, the twenty-two-mile straightaway of U.S. 17, through pines and reeds and fields from South Mills, North Carolina, to Deep Creek, Virginia. The dark Dismal Swamp Canal this road ran beside was the watercourse that tied the Chesapeake to the Albemarle, and for all my growing up I watched the implacable jungle beyond it and heard its simple standard lore: the Swamp was full of runaway slaves and escaped convicts that the law wouldn't follow in. And I was too young at first to understand or have a sense of time before and beyond my own, believing that these slaves and outlaws were there right then, lurking and staring out at me and my family with bad designs from behind the green curtain as the Africans on the riverbank had stared at freshwater sailor Charlie Marlow in Joseph Conrad's tale, "Heart of Darkness."

North beyond all this Swamp was Norfolk, the sprawled-out Navytown queen of Tidewater Virginia, provincial capital for northeastern North Carolina as well. So long allied and tied to each other were Norfolk and our northeast that one Hampton Roads editor, frustrated by decades of conflict with Richmond, hoped in the *Herald* in 1852 that his "people release themselves from bondage by annexing the city, come what may, to North Carolina—who would at least treat us with decent and common justice." We small-town Carolinians loved the whole waterfront shebang that the radio called the "world's greatest harbor," and we loved the big wilderness that lay between us and the city.

On many of the days of my youth, going up to Norfolk to see my Lamborn cousins, up to Norfolk to shop for suits and shoes, my mother behind the wheel of our pale blue Plymouth station wagon, up to Norfolk on the school bus on field trips to the zoo, I, like Conrad's Marlow, had gazed back at that bright darkness and thought his same thought:

When I grow up, I will go there.

Nearly twenty years passed before I got the chance.

One Indian summer in the early 1970s, New Hampshireman John Foley and I went down east out of the Carolina Piedmont, through the last slow rolling hills near Rocky Mount, into the flat uncrowded farm country of the Coastal Plain. In Elizabeth City we intended to rent a canoe or a small skiff, and we failed. The town I remembered was gone—the thriving riverport, the boatbuilding town was no more. No one had small craft to let.

We went into the lobby of the New Southern Hotel, a bloodred brick building at the corner of Road Street and East Main, and started calling around the countryside for outfitters, finally finding one in Virginia Beach. By late afternoon, when we got back to the gateway into the Swamp with our gear, the day had grayed up. We parked our station wagon at the far end of the *Lady of the Lake* tourboat parking lot at Arbuckle Landing, where the wide Feeder Ditch comes down out of the heart of the Swamp and meets the main north and south Canal.

With the same blind homage to the Irish poet that thousands of pilgrims have shown, since his 1803 ballad "The Lake of the Dismal Swamp," we christened our craft the *Tom Moore* and pushed off from the small dock. The Sportsman's Inn, a grill back at the Landing, fell away behind us, and the cries of howling dogs east of the Canalbank faded.

"Looks inviting," Foley said as we passed a ladder overgrown with vines going from water's edge to the top of the high bank, the sides of the deep cut through an ancient oyster reef flecked with white.

We paddled westerly up the shallow canyon at a sprint, because it had been drizzling since we put in and also just to hold our own against the strong current. At dusky dark in a heavy rain we reached the spillway outpost, Waste Weir. On the wooded peninsula on the south side of the Feeder we pitched our tent, got a wet-wood fire going, cooked T-bone steaks and drank Rittenhouse rye, and talked into the night about just where on the face of God's extremely green earth we had gotten ourselves to. Swamp rats, we fancied ourselves.

It was a stormy Monday, and I relished every moment of it. The rain had not let up for more than twenty minutes since we arrived at Waste Weir. Again and again lightning lit up the outpost with blasts of calcium-white light: the small screened and roofed mess hall where we sat, the docks and piers and covered boathouse here on the spit, the spillkeeper's house and garden beyond the spillway.

Each large crack of thunder rolled over the Swamp like a great log rolling over a vast tin ceiling. When we were in the thick of a piece of storm and the lightning was very close, the thunder boomed out with even intensity all around us and receded slowly, echoing all the way, for ten seconds or more after each crash, a slow and marvelous roar.

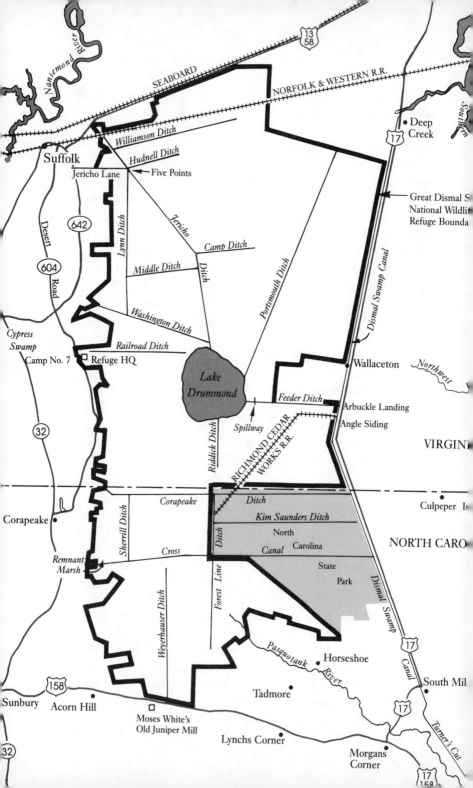

Feeder Ditch at Lake Drummond, outlet locks, about 1890

A little past eleven that first night there was a fairing off, and we left the mess hall to walk around the spill. Frogs were moving, the clouds broke open, and the waxing Harvest Moon shone through. Standing on the spillway itself and looking back down the Feeder was astounding: the ditch was barely visible by moonlight, but when the lightning flashed in the near distance the waterway lit up for a second at a time, a silver strand that seemed to lead straight into a jungled nowhere.

Next morning, the spillwayman hailed us from the house across the ditch, and Foley and I went over and had coffee with him. Almost as soon as he had opened his mouth, speaking in Outer Banks soundside, I asked him,

"Where in Dare County you from?"

"Hatt'ras Oyland," he said, "but Oy been all over Virginia with the Corps of Engineers." His name was Nat Midgette, and he was three shy of thirty years with the Corps. He wore large thick glasses and had both lenses on retirement.

"You be careful bout your fires over there on that point," he said. "We had to pump water down a hole over there, peat fire got started by some coals that was still live. Took two days and we still like not to got it."

This was no small warning. Fires have long deviled the Great Dismal. In 1806 a great fire burned over the Swamp for more than a month. Shinglegetters threw tens of thousands of cypress and juniper shingles into a canal to save them, but the uppermost were above water and they burned away—drenched shingles below them rose to the surface, dried in the heat, and burned as well. An 1839 blaze scorched miles of Swamp in the northwest, and a hunter boating through the same section sixty years later after another big burn there gazed out over thousands of smoldering, smoking acres and called it a charred desert.

So the record went, and worsened: the 1923 fire that burned for three years over a hundred and fifty square miles; the latesummer fires of 1930 that burned over a thousand acres each and the October fire that fall that burned ten thousand acres before November rains put it out; fires burning at will in the Swamp all through the Great Depression after all parties, all agencies gave up; the deep peat fires of 1941 and 1942 that clouded the coastline so badly that Hampton Roads was endangered—little traffic of any sort could move, including the U-boat patrols offshore—and it took the Army and the Navy and the governors of Carolina and Virginia to make the war effort put out the fire in the Swamp.

But Nat Midgette didn't have to read the whole record to Foley and me that first morning over coffee, for all that too was Great Dismal lore I'd long heard, of firefighters disappearing into flaming pits where the peat had burned out from beneath them and they had fallen through the top crust, of pinetops exploding like fireworks and cascading high over plowed firelanes to ignite the heated, waiting woods beyond. We would be careful about our fires over there on the point.

The soundsider watched as we unhitched our canoe and paddled around the point, up through the profusion of yellow cowlilies all abloom around the banks. At the head of the lagoon was a boat railway, once driven by hand winch and now by motor, for moving small craft from the Feeder Ditch level below the spillway to the Lake level above.

We dragged the canoe up the railway to the higher water, and, as we started on in, Nat Midgette called after us:

"It says be back by six, but you all come on back from the Lake whenever you want to."

The sun was burning off a heavy mist from the storm and the night, and the air was cotton thick, dishrag damp. Foley in the bow spotted catbirds and bluejays, and a loon led us on up the ditch, whose banks were now even with the water. Ahead of us in heavy-laden grapevines and in wild hedges of brilliant orange jewelweed the loon would alight, awaiting us and then moving out of the tunnel of trees and into the light of the Lake.

Lake Drummond, Drummond's Pond, was placid but not glassy as we pulled and paddled to the great cypress at the Feeder's mouth. The far shores all reflected and shimmered through the remaining light mist, and it was impossible to focus.

Only then, as it glided across the Lake away from us, did the loon cry out.

⇐

William Drummond, a Scot and a lawyer, came down from Virginia in the fall of 1664, with official papers on him: he was by appointment of the Lords Proprietors, the owners, the first governor of North Carolina. There weren't fifteen hundred people in Carolina to govern, tax, charge rents, or get paid by, so Governor Drummond for salary got the sole trade in furs for three years.

In 1665, under a large oak tree on Halls Creek in southwestern Pasquotank County, the new governor convened the first Carolina council, an open-air legislature called the Assembly of Albemarle. Here the assemblymen resolved to ask the Lords Proprietors to let them pay the same land rents as Virginians did, instead of twice as much, and they resolved too that "the members should wear shoes, if not stockings, during the session and that they must not throw their chicken and other bones under the tree." There is little record of what else they did.

That same year Governor Drummond and two or three others hunted the Great Dismal Swamp, got themselves lost, stumbled upon the large dark lake at the heart of the Swamp, and all but the governor perished there. After days of wandering, Drummond alone found his way back out, ragged and starving and raving a report of the great lake. Or perhaps none of this happened at all, for there is no record of this either, beyond published and republished hearsay.

What did occur was continued immigration to Carolina, from Virginia and New England and the Indies, and, despite that, displeasure towards Drummond among the Lords Proprietors. By 1667 he was out of favor and out of office.

William Drummond returned to Virginia, which had been ruled for years by a militant royalist and malevolent despot named William Berkeley. Originally appointed governor of Virginia by Charles I in 1641, Berkeley was still refusing to recognize Cromwell's Commonwealth when a Puritan militia showed up in Virginia and deposed him three years after the king's beheading.

It was Berkeley, serving again as governor under Charles II, who engineered both Drummond's appointment and retirement, and it was Berkeley against whom Drummond worked as Virginia collapsed into civil war in the 1670s. High taxes, low tobacco prices, and the cavalier venality of Governor Berkeley's close associates had soured the spirit of the colony, and Indian trouble on the Virginia frontier made the yeomen fighting mad.

Berkeley refused to help the men on the fringe, and Nathaniel Bacon, well-born kinsman of the seventeenth-century scientific theorist Francis Bacon, became champion of the frontiersmen— Bacon led two successful sallies against the Indians, got elected to the House of Burgesses, and got arrested by Governor Berkeley when he came to Jamestown to take his seat. But Bacon got out and gathered his rabble, pressuring the governor into letting him keep on with his Indian campaigns.

The Burgesses voted reform, and Berkeley fled to the Eastern Shore, until he could raise a force and return and proclaim Bacon a treasonous rebel. Bacon fought the governor for the capital, and won. Berkeley fled again, but now Bacon feared he could not hold Jamestown, and he and his people put the torch to the town.

William Drummond burned his own house. Through it all, the former Carolina governor had been one of Bacon's closest advisers, who when warned of the danger of this collaboration said: "I am in over shoes, I had as well be over boots."

By October 1676, the twenty-nine-year-old Bacon controlled the colony of Virginia. No one controls from the colony of the dead, though, and when malaria put him there that month, Bacon's Rebellion fell apart.

Now Berkeley came back with a mind for vengeance. Though Charles II had authorized Berkeley to grant full pardon to all rebels except Bacon, with no one else to be excluded, Berkeley dismissed the order and went about his bloody business.

They captured William Drummond in Chickahominy Swamp in January 1677, and brought him before the governor. When Berkeley saw the prisoner he bowed contemptuously low to him, and gave away his great pleasure and hatred when he said:

"Mister Drummond, you are very welcome. I am more glad to see you than any man in Virginia. Mister Drummond, you shall be hanged in half an hour."

"What your honor pleases," Drummond replied.

His captors paid the former governor these rough respects: they ripped his ring from his finger, stripped him, clapped him in irons, threw him into a ship's brig at King's Creek, and set him trudging next morning still shackled and ill-clothed five bittercold miles to Middle Plantation, now Williamsburg. His guards let him stop and have a pipe, and one of them made him an offer:

"Sir, would you like a horse, to ride the rest of the way?"

"No, thank you," said Governor Drummond. "I shall walk to my death soon enough."

Governor Berkeley rolled in by carriage, met Drummond at midday and, refusing him any self-defense, condemned him again in short order to the gallows that afternoon at four. Then Berkeley seized Sarah Drummond's property, and left the governor's widow and five small children to wander the Virginia woods fearing for their own lives and practically starving as they fled and hid. Berkeley kept on plundering, oversaw more revenge killings, and disobeyed for as long as he could the king's orders to quit Virginia and return home and explain the commotions. Ill and exhausted and mortified when he finally arrived in England to face the king, he died before he could do so, his wretched heart and spirit broken at last.

"That old fool," Charles II declared, "has put more people to death in that naked country than I did for the murder of my father."

Back in the Virginia wilderness, a lonely lovely ruby-water pond soon bore the governor-rebel's name:

Lake Drummond.

⮜

That first morning on the Lake, it took only another quarter hour after we'd canoed out onto it for the hot September sun to steam Drummond clean and clear. The broad pear-shaped Lake is slightly less than two and a half miles across, east to west, slightly more than that north to south. After the mist cleared, we headed north along the Lake's eastern shore.

Up Portsmouth Ditch on the northeast side we nearly plowed into a watersnake sunning itself in the dappled light on an earthen spillway. This was the only snake we saw the whole week we were encamped in the Swamp, but we backed away from it quickly as if it were a moccasin and the harbinger of a hive of its confederates. We ate sandwiches out on a dock at the mouth of Portsmouth Ditch, a channel foolishly cut into Drummond in the 1890s by citizens of Portsmouth mistakenly believing they could use the Lake as their reservoir. $90,000 shot to hell.

On towards Jericho Ditch, on the Lake's northwest side, we plied after lunch, passing charred piling tops where a cabin above had apparently burned, tying up a half-hour in a colony of cypress offshore while we waited for a wind to die down. There were three cabins on piers over the water and one on the land between Portsmouth and Jericho.

Porte Crayon's Lake Drummond, *1856*

At a small sandy beach on the north shore we ran aground. It was hot now, and I heard two men working on the next cottage west of us, one complaining to the other about poison ivy growing up the side of the house. Something was at work growing everywhere: moss caps on old stumps in the shallows, flowers and weeds on logs all around the Lake, the dense maple and cypress jungle encircling us. In the water were small slivers of wood, and there at the north beach were many pieces of waterworn cypress, saturated and sunk and lying in the sand under water.

The whole Lake would be ours by dusk. As another wind picked up, we cut south to Riddick Ditch, passing through the center of shallow Drummond about four o'clock. The cove at Riddick's had two great cypress guards, and a large cypress log lay hollowed and half submerged at the end of a tumbledown pier. Each time a wave slammed up inside it, an amber froth blew forth through a small hole in the log like whale spume.

It was a short distance from Riddick's back to the Feeder, but it took us forty-five minutes against a stout crosswind to make the pull.

Back at the spillway just past six, big stolid Corpsman Jones was hauling a government skiff up the boat railway to flip it and get the bottom ready to paint.

"You should of talked to old Cap'n Crockett," Jones said. "He could tell you a thing or two about this Swamp."

William Crockett was a sailor, a fisherman, a timberman, who about 1930 came to the Great Dismal from the Eastern Shore of Maryland, lived on the Canalbank Highway, and guided people in and out of the Swamp from his landing there. The outfitter up in Virginia Beach had said to Foley and me: "He'd greet you at his landing even if you were putting in at five-thirty, six A.M. Come out, lean back, look at the sky and say, 'Guess it's okay for you boys to go on her but nobody else better today—by midafternoon there'll be two-and-a-half-, three-foot waves on the east shore.' You could have put a tape measure to those waves, Crockett wouldn't be off more'n a inch."

It was Cap'n Crockett—a kinsman, by his own reckoning, of frontiersman Davy Crockett—who led the naturalist Edwin Way Teale and his wife Nellie on the Lake Drummond leg of the Teales' famed "North with the Spring" journey a few years after World War II, and who, having brought them in on a blue May day when a swarm of golden-banded honeybees had been windblown and scattered over the Lake, chanted out if not sang to them the whole of Thomas Moore's Dismal poem:

A Ballad

The Lake of the Dismal Swamp

Written at Norfolk, In Virginia

"They made her a grave too cold and damp
  For a soul so warm and true;
And she's gone to the lake of the Dismal Swamp
Where all night long, by a firefly lamp,
  She paddles her white canoe.

"And her firefly lamp I soon shall see,
  And her paddle I soon shall hear;
Long and loving our life shall be,

And I'll hide the maid in a cypress tree,
   When the footstep of death is near!"

Away to the Dismal Swamp he speeds;
   His path was rugged and sore;
Through tangled juniper, beds of reeds,
Through many a fen, where the serpent feeds,
   And man never trod before.

And when on the earth he sank to sleep,
   If slumber his eyelids knew,
He lay where the deadly vine doth weep,
Its venomous tear and nightly steep,
   The flesh with blistering dew!

And near him the she-wolf stirred the brake,
   And the copper snake breathed in his ear,
Till he starting cried, from his dream awake,
"Oh, when shall I see the dusky lake,
   And the white canoe of my dear?"

He saw the lake and a meteor bright
   Quick over its surface played—
"Welcome!" he said; "my dear one's light";
And the dim shore echoed for many a night,
   The name of the death-cold maid.

Till he hollowed a boat of the birchen bark,
   Which carried him off from shore;
Far he followed the meteor spark;
The wind was high and the clouds were dark,
   And the boat returned no more.

But oft from the Indian hunter's camp,
   This lover and maid so true,
Are seen at the hour of midnight damp,
To cross the lake by a firefly lamp,
   And paddle their white canoe.

On the highway in front of his house, the old balladeer was killed,
run down by a car. "Lotta stories been wrote down that Crockett

told," Jones went on, scraping away on his skiff. "He knew this Swamp."

When I suggested that Jones himself might know a thing or two about the Great Dismal, he said:

"History ain't to my liking. It was my sorry subject when I was in school." Then, eyeing us confidentially, he allowed, "I think ol' George Washington was a busy man if he done all the things they say he done."

"And Martha she done got left out," said Jones's sidekick Frank, a friendly and wheezy old Swamper who was a ward of the spillway keepers.

"You lucky it's the black fly now, 'stead of the yellow fly," Jones said, sweating heavily and slapping at them more vigorously than he'd been scraping the hull. "Frank, I believe I'm gon give this boat up for a bad job."

After a fine hash and beans dinner, Foley and I went over to the spillkeeper's house and got to talking again. Jones looked at our old USGS map and let us know in short order that there were a lot more ditches in the Swamp than our map showed. Why you could get to this one from that one if you turned twice, and on and on like that he went, letting us know how little we knew, and Frank scarcely had the time to say:

"You could walk right over Riddick's Ditch in 1940 and not even know it."

When he was fully convinced he'd done all he could to beat back our ignorance, Jones said goodbye—he was off till the end of the week—and we listened as he fired up his boat and took off, ripping down the Feeder Ditch in the bright dark, moonlight and longtime habit guiding him home.

&

Later we paddled slowly out the Feeder onto Drummond by night and tied up to an old weir stake a couple hundred feet straight out into the Lake. The Harvest Moon rolled slowly across the September sky, and the Lake was calm under it, a light breeze and just a hint of a mist. Faraway on the north shore was a single light, from the hunters' cabin called "Lady of the Lake." For a good long while we didn't speak, just listened to locusts and crickets and frogs in the dark woods rimmed around us and to the dark water lapping at the little metal boat.

The Lake is young as natural lakes go, no more than four thousand years old, and it is simpler to say what did not form it than to say what did. It is not a meteor crater full of water, nor the last bit of an open-water swamp. It is not a Carolina bay, for these elliptical depressions in the Carolina lowlands formed during the Ice Age, not after it, as Drummond did. Perhaps its bottom simply collapsed, as the sink-holes do in Florida, or perhaps a fire deep in the peat left this shallow saucer to fill with juniper water long remarked and bragged upon.

Drummond's water is famous, for it would stay fresh a year or more, full of tannic acid as it is. Our Navy in the nineteenth century had an iron-hulled tanker built, the *Water Witch*, to run up to Drummond and fill up and bring good fresh Dismal Swamp water back to supply the fleet. But the *Water Witch* was too stout to get through the Deep Creek locks. Even so, they say Admiral Matthew Perry carried casks of this water to Japan on his Pacific Overtures trip in 1853.

It is the color of tea, madeira, port, brandy, bourbon, ruby, chocolate, blood, folks say. My friend Homer Foil told me it looked to him like black-bean soup, another comrade said Killian's Red Ale. John Foley and I drank a lot of it while we were there that week, chased the rye with it as we lolled in the canoe that night under the moon. "Rainwater sweet," Foley said of it.

"Who cooks for you?"

The first barred owl's cry broke the spell.

"Who cooks for you-all?"

At least two of them were calling back and forth, but it was hard to pinpoint where they were, their cries so filled the woods and the empty edge of the Lake. I replied, and my own echo came back at us greatly amplified. I gave the gunwale a sharp rap, a flat slap of my hand, and it was a rifle shot on its return.

Bats, which live and breed in the empty cypress stumps in the Lake, had been out all evening, but now they began to dart close, cutting across the canoe and around our heads. We called it a night and headed on in to the spillway, all lit up across the top with a string of lights. These glistened in the dark Swamp night, and they reflected glittering off the dark waters. It was like coming upon a riverboat lodged up some bayou, with a Cajun ball just underway.

Mornings that week were oppressively damp, and a light rain was usually falling by eight. An old dog was always wandering around the spillway compound, a dog that looked like a worn black rug with white trim.

"He keeps the bears away," Nat Midgette told us. "Been here all his life, and bears don't like it when a dog gets to barking."

We would slip out to the Lake, work our way along the shores, and slide back into the spillway when it got too windy and choppy on Drummond. The Lake had been calm for us only three times: on first viewing, at the north beach, and under the moon that first night. Rain would fall heavily, then slack off, then stop, and then repeat the cycle. Even when the rain ceased a while, water was hanging in the cotton-thick air, and, with a slight wind and the temperature about sixty, the Swamp kept throwing a real chill into us.

Once a day the *Lady of the Lake* tourboat scooted up the Feeder, transferred its tourists to an upperlevel craft—the *Jungle Queen*—and then this second craft came out upon the Lake for fifteen or twenty minutes. No one else had come to the spillway since Foley and I arrived days before, just us and Nat Midgette the soundsider and Jones the boatscraper and Frank the swamp rat. And a fourth man, also a Corpsman, a young fellow from Elizabeth City named Tisdale.

One night Tisdale bragged on Drummond's catfish and crappie and bemoaned its few bream and rare bass. "And there's no ducks," he said. "Nothing for them to feed on back here. But they come in aplenty to feed in that pond north side of the Feeder Ditch back towards the Landing, near the cornfields."

Cypress trees, eastern Lake Drummond, 1880s

We talked about how far out Drummond remained so very shallow, two or three feet deep at as much as a hundred yards from shore, and how in all that shallow field was a webbing of cypress roots and old stumps, a natural tangled mess. Many droughts, heavy draining too through the Feeder, have revealed this dark mesh time and again.

"We'd drain her all the way if we had to, to keep the Canal level up," Tisdale said. "We got it so low once you couldn't motor out of the Feeder Ditch onto Drummond." He knew Foley and I had been out onto the Lake at night, and he warned us:

"Listen, it's bad to get out there in a fog, I can tell you, I been messed up with it."

Then his shift was over, and he fired off down the Feeder in the Corps' small-cabined launch, running it blind like the others but every now and again flashing his white spotlight ahead to warn anyone who might for some unimaginable reason have strayed up the ditch at ten o'clock at night.

Soon he and the high urgent grind of the launch were gone, and a thick mist began rolling up to the spillway from Lake Drummond. By midnight, another wild storm was lashing the Great Dismal.

Old Frank was out in the cucumber patch early the next morning, wheezing and coughing, but coming out with a bucket full of cukes. Raccoons or possums had knocked over several garbage cans, and some critter had gotten to some chocolate we thought we had well hid. Nat Midgette and two other men were working on the top of the *Jungle Queen*, for last night's big wind had stove in its roof.

Out on Drummond the air was clear. A moderate wind was up, and there was no haze. Yesterday's view of the far shores was that of a shoreline during light snow, but now the wall of green woods across the way stood plain and unmysterious.

We broke camp on the fifth day, followed a heron and a hawk down the Feeder out from the heart of the Great Dismal, back to the Canalbank Highway and the Sportsman's Inn. Inside the little grill we had a hot dog and a beer, and talked to Ed the owner until Tisdale came in and sat at the counter with us, just killing time before running up the Feeder to work.

"What's the story on Frank?" I said.

"Well, Frank's been in the Swamp all his life," said Tisdale.

"Ever work?"

"No, I don't think Frank ever hurt hisself much."

Ed laughed, and said Frank was really fond of Tisdale, that he would always follow Tisdale's lead. "I bought a whole box of Blue Ribbon cigars for Frank cause that's what he smoked. Then he comes in here to cash in bottles he's gathered up at the Lake. Says, 'Forget the money—gimme some of them King Edwards.' I asked him about the Blue Ribbons he used to like and he said, 'No, Tisdale smokes King Edwards so I'm going to too.'"

"Well," Tisdale said, "I saw a bunch of Blue Ribbons on the table up there at the spillway, and I asked him what about them when Frank wanted to bum one of my King Edwards. And he said, 'Oh, that's just what old Ed stuck me with.'"

I remember we bought a King Edward off Ed, to send back up to Frank by way of Tisdale. I knew that someday I would see Drummond's Pond again, even if it were a long time, but I knew that we had seen the last of the old coughing man with the black-rug dog out

Porte Crayon's Camp on the Lake, *1856*

in the Swamp cucumber patch. Tisdale took the cigar and tapped the air with it a time or two and nodded because he knew the old man would appreciate the smoke, and the nod was thanking us on Frank's behalf. And just before we left he said:

"Frank's about had it with the Swamp." Then he sat still for a few moments and refigured the thought, and when he spoke again he paid his respects to the far greater force:

"Yeah, the Swamp's about got old Frank."

🐸

2

Juniper

"*Cedar*, a sweet wood good for seelings, Chests, boxes, Bedsteedes, Lutes, Virginals, and many things els, as I have also said before. Some of our company which have wandered in some places where I have not bene, have made certaine affirmation of *Cyprus* which for such and other excellent uses, is also a wood of price and no small estimation."—Thomas Harriot, *A Briefe and True Report of the New Found Land of Virginia*, London, February 1588

 One broiling August afternoon twelve years after my Swamping with John Foley, I sat down at the South Mills Restaurant—itself set just a few feet from the Dismal Swamp Canal's lower locks—to a cheeseburger as big as a hubcap. It was just past two, and the half dozen pine booths and five stools at the counter were all empty. A sign on the wall showed in wintry sunset silhouette a man with a rifle and a stag in tall timber, and the legend was simply, "After the hunt, Budweiser."

Until 1839 South Mills was New Lebanon, named by Bible-minded people inspired by the great stately Atlantic white cedars, or juniper, that throve in vast stretches of the Swamp all around them. There were in 1800 two timber companies hereabouts, Old and New Lebanon, most of whose overlapping shareholders were north-eastern North Carolinians, though businessmen from as far away as Philadelphia and South Carolina were drawn into the Lebanon cedar trade.

New Lebanon, the timber concern, claimed around twenty-four thousand acres along the Dismal Swamp Canal, and this before the first shingle lighter ever floated upon it. Old Lebanon had some forty or fifty thousand acres a ways west, where the headwaters of

South Mills, N.C., on the Dismal Swamp Canal, about 1910

Pasquotank River flowed down out of the Swamp through the old community of Newfoundland, now Horseshoe. By 1930, these and other timbermen would cut over a hundred thousand acres of juniper out of this great Swamp.

I had just spent the past five hours circumnavigating the Great Dismal. My way into Swamp country that day was through the Sand Banks east of Chowan River, where sheep grazed behind a fenced-in branch of swamp and big cutout wooden letters far beyond the flock spelled ISRAEL and JESUS. U.S. 158 east of Tarheel is shot straight, and the road gave back a fast quarter-note rhythm as my tires clipped over the tarjoints in the highway. At tiny Sunbury the crepe myrtle was in bloom in force, and at tinier Acorn Hill the paint was long gone from the clapboards of closed-up Lucille's Place and a busted thermometer on the worn wall was pegging a hundred and one. Morning glories twined around cornstalks, and the lower branches of trees reached out to the road like beckoning hands and arms. Soybeans were chest high, buttercups ran wild alongside the road, and vast pine stands and mixed woods stood at the broad-field edges like great mountainheads, a summer haze hanging in it all.

From Corapeake I drove into Virginia on the Desert Road, up

along the sandy Suffolk Scarp, or Nansemond Escarpment, the Pleistocene seabeach that stretches two hundred miles, from the Potomac River south to the Neuse in Carolina. Down the side of the Scarp peanut fields go rolling off into the Swamp, ending at the big woods. Then I had come around the top end of the Swamp, from Suffolk back over to Deep Creek, the brawling payday town of the oldtime shinglers and swampers, and down the Canalbank once more. The waterlevel in the Canal was way down, the Canal was closed to boat traffic, and there were sandy beaches down both its sides.

I meandered east on Ballahack Road, climbed an untended and shaky firetower and gazed out on hundreds of acres of corn near Wallaceton, then headed over to Moyock and a haunt from my boyhood—the old dog-racing track there, where my mother won a set of crystal-draped candleholders just after the War. The oval raceway was being reclaimed by weeds and willows and even a line of myrtles, and all that was left of the grandstand was its concrete base. A dozen appliances were out in the weather, and there were rusted girders and rivets all around. A mile and a half north, my sisters and cousins and I used to straddle the Carolina and Virginia line and loudly proclaim to the heavens that we were in two states at the same time, two places at once. Now, nearby, a Wollenweber antenna—one hundred telephone poles nearly a hundred feet tall and all strung with wires in a circular clearing—pulls in for the hungry ears of Naval Intelligence conversations between tanks out in the Saudi Arabian desert. *Sic semper innocentiae.*

Along and over Shingle Landing Creek I went on 1227, from Moyock curving back to South Mills, passing a car pulling a trailer of corn in thin-slat boxes, the shucks hanging and flapping out through the slats in the breeze. Beyond Stingy Lane and below Tar Corner—named for a tar-painted barn—a report on McCoy's Store said "Gone Out of Business." A handtruck stood idle out front, and an Orange Crush metal bottle sign was flaking away on the wall.

At Morgans Corner, just outside South Mills, I stopped for gas at a station across from Carver's Fish Store and Shoe Shop. The pumpboy smiled in the stifling heat and said:

"Hot enough for you?"

"No," I said, "I like it hotter."

"Damn if I do."

And hotter I would get it, in just a few minutes more, disappearing into the Great Dismal once again, this time from the south and by car with an old friend of my father's. Nowhere yet this day had I seen a stick of juniper, but the old man on Upriver Road knew where the last of it was.

⨭

Reggie Gregory was out in his barn working on a broken-down tractor. He had promised a man he'd saw some timber for him on the little sawmill in his backyard, but the tractor powered the mill and it had had them foxed all day.

"Thought it was the water pump," he said to me, after I had walked up and stood outside the work circle he and several other men formed. "Pulled it, put it back, tractor's still losing water— turned out to be the freeze plugs in the damn thing."

Beyond the big oaks and the barn and the broad lawn, not a hundred feet past his two-story frame farmhouse and his sawmill, the Swamp began. Reggie scrubbed the grease off his arms out in the yard and waved that way, inviting the disappointed man whose timber had gone unsawn to come along with us.

"Naw, Reggie," he said, "I ain't interested in going back in that Swamp. You go on without me."

Up a broad grass roadway between ditches and fields we drove into the Swamp, the two of us in my front-wheel-drive station wagon. Now it was past four o'clock, the air still and close in the middle nineties, and we were going now because Reggie had said, "It's too damn hot in the Swamp in the middle of the day."

Of the wide road he remarked, "We built this airstrip when I was with the Forest Service. During World War II, the government hired me to look after the Dismal Swamp, keep the fire out of there on account of the smoke—they wasn't interested in saving the timber. It was just on account of the smoke, it was bothering the boys flying the planes on the coast down here. And they hired me: I was the Dismal Swamp Ranger.

"And I hired about forty men, I reckon, to work just temporarily with me. They lived right home, wasn't supposed to do anything till I called em to a fire. Then they were supposed to drop what they were doing and come help me. I think we paid em about eighty, hundred dollars a month. Had em in Camden, Currituck, down in Dare, all around.

"The state bought some War planes, converted them into tankers—they'd hold three hundred gallons of water and chemicals. We had three, four of em down here. And we had portable mixing tanks that we'd bring over here to this airstrip and set em up. I know one time we had a fire back there in the Swamp on the Corapeake Road, and we mixed and loaded here on this airstrip. They were dumping a load of water every three minutes on that fire.

"And then after the War was over, the government quit that. I went to come back on the farm, and then later on I got a job at the Forest Service, as a district forest ranger, and I stayed there till I was sixty-five and a half, and retired. Still lived here at the farm."

The airstrip ended and the road narrowed, and the Swamp woods yanked right up next to us. At a massive iron gate we stopped, and Reggie got out and went and unlocked the Great Dismal. He gave the gate a good strong shove and waved me through as it swung open. Beneath his feedstore cap his long face was all a-sweat, and his dark green workpants were the color of the jungle we were entering. He was pushing eighty, but Reggie was so sturdy and resolute and at home that he didn't look much more than sixty.

"When I was a boy," Reggie said as we rode on, "I'd leave home in the dark, before day, come back in here and work my traplines, wearing hip boots, walking in water up to my knees all day, get back home about dark. In here alone all day, nobody knowing where I was. What if I'd sprained a ankle? Could of been it. You know, that was stupid!"

So he said now. But fifty years ago, by the time he was in his mid-twenties, Reggie Gregory was running a line of three hundred end-spring Victor traps spread out over a fifteen-mile round trip through the southern Great Dismal. "And I'd make that trip about three times a week. I did that for about eight years, that's where I made the biggest part of my living.

"But I wasn't the only one. A lot of the other fellows up here that was farming did the same thing. A whole lot of em would of lost their little farms if it hadn't been for this Swamp. There was twenty, twenty-five people doing the same thing, right in this section. On the Gates County side, I don't know how many was trapping in there cause back in those days we didn't go on the other side of the Swamp much. That was way way from home when you got over on that side of the Swamp."

Reggie remembered Depression soybeans going for fifty cents a bushel, corn for a quarter. Farm labor paid a dollar a day. "And I could go back in that Swamp and catch a mink, and get seven dollars for him. I would catch seven, eight, sometimes ten minks a week. Coonskins was from three to five dollars.

"Duck Glover in Elizabeth City was the main man, the main buyer. He would skin em, scrape em, clean em up, and he carried em to New York and sold em up there."

When minks went high, sometimes up to ten and fifteen dollars apiece, the local buyers didn't wait in country stores or remote outposts for the trappers to bring the fur to them. "There was another fellow, I can't remember his name, but he was a Jew out of Virginia. He'd find your car where you'd parked, or mule and cart, whatever you drove up to the Swamp, and he'd sit *there* and wait for you to come back. I've come out there lots of times and he paid me a hundred dollars for that day's work, and that's more money than I got off the farm the whole year. So if it hadn't been for that old Swamp, you see what kind of shape I'd of been in, and a lot of my friends would of been in. That's why I hate to see it closed down, where we can't use it."

Some of Reggie's steel traps are in the Swamp yet. Every year when trapping ended he gathered them all up and hid them in a hollow log until the next season. He thought about that a minute and said, "As far as I know they're still there."

"Could you go to that log?" I asked him.

"No," he said, admitting the changes in the landscape and in himself, "I couldn't find that log today."

Not quite half a mile below Arbuckle Landing out on the main Canal was Angle Siding, the upper terminus of the Richmond Cedar Works railroad. From here the trainline, a forty-two-inch gauge, took off into the Swamp, running westerly about a mile and a quarter, then cutting southwest at a forty-five-degree angle on down into North Carolina for five miles, making another sharp turn and heading due south for five more miles. The timbermen built a trestle for their train, then went back and filled it in with earth in hopes this muckmire causeway would stay stable.

From the early 1900s till about 1940 Cedar Works logged the Swamp of its juniper and its cypress, and for some of that time my grandfather Simpson did legal work for the company. I inherited two shares of Richmond Cedar Works stock, and, though the concern is now only a local legend and the name on a defunct file in a New York lawyer's office, my children walk on floors and sleep beneath a cottage roof that Cedar Works timber helped pay for.

All that remains of the company in the Swamp is its old railroad grade.

Reggie and I stopped twice to take a look at it, see what was left. The first time was at a point where the Camden and Pasquotank County-line ditch crossed it. Anyone moving at more than two or three miles an hour and not looking for it anyway would have never seen the railway or, seeing it, would not have given it a second thought.

The trees were all arched and intertwined above it, and it was now a tunnel into a green oblivion, into an arbor gone mad and wild. I stood there on the County Line Road and stared north into this dim tube, but it was almost all in shadows, its dark vanishing point none too distant. Light traffic now, whitetail deer and few bear, where a forty-ton steam engine and all its burden once thundered through.

"It pulled a hundred cars," Reggie said. "Carried a hundred carloads of logs when it went out. It was a big train."

And there was big timber going out on it, had been for fifteen years or so before Reggie Gregory and his cohort trappers from the southern Dismal started to see the Cedar Works up close. "You see, they started over on the other side of the Swamp, and I didn't know much about what was going on till they come and had the road built clean through out here to where the switches come out and we could get in the switches and go to the main line. And then they logged in there for fifteen, twenty years after I got big enough to go in there and know what they was doing."

The switches were spurs every couple hundred yards on either side of the main grade, down which smaller engines, dinkies, ran the logcars to collect the bounteous plunder of the wilderness. "Old Fordson tractors," Reggie recalled their using along the switches. They ran portable bunkhouses, eight-by-sixteen–foot camp buildings down these sidings, too, for the men who worked the logwoods.

"All that juniper back in there was so thick," he went on, "you had to throw ever tree the same way, you couldn't throw em back. Men would roll em out to the roads, then roll em up poles to them cars, put down two poles up on the car, and a man'd get at each end, maybe one in the middle, and roll em up on the car. That's the way they loaded em, paid em so much a carload. Didn't even have a skidder—couldn't put a skidder in there cause it was so thick.

"They cut it with crosscut saws. Richmond Cedar Works and Roper Lumber Company didn't use any power saws when they cut this Swamp out the first time. They wasn't even in existence. They had saws made extra long, cause they couldn't cut em with ordinary crosscut saws. Trees so big. I've seen hollow cypress back there where they'd cut the tree, and the first log'd be hollow and they'd just leave it lying there where it fell. I'm six foot tall, and I could walk right in that log and not even bow my head sixteen feet one end to the other. And a lot of those cypress were solid through now. I've seen car after car come out of there with one log onto it, with a little log on each side of it to chock it. Cypress logs, one log on a car. It'd be four, five foot diameter, at the little end."

Though he never worked for a timber company, Reggie Gregory

ran a train all his own back in the Swamp. He and his brother had a pump-car they rode into the Great Dismal on weekends. "They were almost never in here on Saturdays, never on Sundays." Later on he built a small train car, powered by a Briggs and Stratton engine and set upon old truck rims, to carry his friends in to hunt, pulling a dog-cart behind.

"Sometimes we *would* see the train," he said.

"What would you do?" I asked.

"We'd all jump off, throw that car of ours off to the side. Get out the *way*!"

⪜

The Cedar Works railroad hits the Forest Line Road about a mile below the Carolina and Virginia border, and there in the cedar thicket on both sides of the sandy lane we stopped again.

In close ranks the cedar spires stand, each tree a tall tawny pole with bark in thin vertical strips marking a slow swirling whorl around and about the tree up to its dark green arrow-crown. They grow in a thick, high-acid peat of their own making and reach heights of sixty and seventy feet, diameters of a foot. Deadfalls and windfalls cross and lap each other on the forest floor, and walking in the cedars is slow going, or no going at all. A watercolorist touring the cedar thicket on Camp Ditch, two or three miles north of Lake Drummond, called the color of the cedars' high crowns thalo-cyanine green—the coldest, darkest green on the palette—and said the shade they cast was a dark shade. Only wood thrush and bluejay usually breed in the cedar woods, though in winter pine siskins by the thousands will feed on the little juniper cones. In aerial photographs, the Swamp's few remaining patches of cedar show up stark and dramatic, like shadows on the moon.

"Well," Reggie said, "there's your juniper."

We left the car and stumbled into the woods, and here the railroad grade was just an elongated mound a foot or two above the forest floor and all grown up in cedars. Only an old Swamper could have

Juniper

gone right to it, for from the Forest Line Road it was indistinguishable from the rest of the juniper thicket.

"Looka here," he said, and called me over to a cedar he was studying. "They caught em a bear here. See, they had their trap chained onto this tree right here, and you can see how the bear worked at it, yanked on it, dug the chain in, made them marks there. Old bear didn't like it one bit."

Just beyond the tree we'd been studying was a four-inch juniper sapling that the angry, fettered bear had broken off and splintered at about chest height. "No," Reggie said again, "bear don't like to be held up. Well, that's some more of the old railroad, all's left of it."

Up the road apiece we ran across the bear man, Eric Hellgren, an ingenuous curly-haired and freckle-faced fellow in his twenties roaring about the Swamp roads on a red four-wheeler all-terrain contraption. He was busy catching black bears for a study run by Virginia Polytechnic Institute, then setting them loose with radio collars and tracking their Great Dismal peregrinations, picking up their bruin broadcasts with a portable radio and a directional H antenna that looked like a toaster-oven element on a handle and that he held aloft and waved all around as he made his own daily pilgrimages through the Swamp.

"Just caught our sixty-fifth bear this afternoon, a little fifty-five pound girl," Eric told us excitedly. Eventually they would catch and tag a hundred and one, reckoning the Swamp as home to two hundred and sixty. In his recent survey *The Great Cypress Swamps*, John Dennis ranked the Dismal's bear population as one of the primary three on the East Coast, along with those in North Carolina's Alligator River swamps and in Georgia's Okefenokee.

Eric said that the bears had been feeding on black cherry but now were hitting the pokeweed that grew along the ditchbanks and roadsides. As we drove on, east along Corapeake Ditch, we saw many places where the lanky, ink-berried pokeweed was knocked over onto the road, and then, about forty yards up the lane from us, we saw a small bear. I stopped, and the bear stuck its nose high into the air, worked it about, looked at us, then bolted about ten or fifteen yards farther down the road. It looked back at us while I grabbed a camera, and right when I was ready, it dove south into the Swamp and disappeared.

"You won't see him no more—he's gone," said Reggie.

The Gregory family, like many families farming the margins of the Great Dismal, once had big trouble with bears tearing up their crops. One year the bears were so thick he said it always looked like cattle had been in their corn. They killed twenty-seven bears, right there in the field, some of them as heavy as four hundred pounds. Sometimes men sat up on stands waiting for the bears to leave the Swamp and enter the fields. Sometimes they set trip-wire shotguns, loaded with double-ought buckshot, slugs, or, as Reggie said, "Anything we could get." One farmer he knew stoked up a muzzleloader with a leg broken off of a cast-iron pot. "He'd kill a bear and take it out, load it in his gun again, set it again—fellow killed four bears with the same pot-leg."

There were bearhunters, too, who went after the bears on their own account or working for farmers or even as guides. The Temple brothers, Billy Ed and Cortez, were the best known of these. They ran dogs after the bear, and they led pilots from Langley Field—who used to fly down and land in a cowpasture—to the hunt.

"When I'd catch seven, eight coons a day," Reggie said, "well, I couldn't bring all them coons out, so I'd just skin em, put the fur in my coat and throw the coon away. And the bears knew that and they'd follow behind me and eat them coons. And I could hear em coming behind me, and they round the line waiting for me, I reckon. I didn't even have a gun. I've seen em walking right behind me, I don't know if they're walking behind me to get the coons, or to get *me*. I seen as high as three and four at a time."

One night out coon hunting just off the Cedar Works railroad's main line, Reggie's hound treed and Reggie took off from the railroad into the Swamp with his two-cell flashlight and single-shot .22 rifle. The understory and brambles were so thick he ended up crawling to get to the dog, which was sounding off with his feet up on a big gum. Reggie stood to shine the light and shoot the coon out of the tree, but the coon was a two-hundred-fifty-pound bear about ten or twelve feet up the tree. It slammed the treetrunk right over

Reggie's head and sent him scrambling, and he went back to the railroad and got a shotgun from the black man he was hunting with, then returned to the gumtree and fired at the bear.

"Now, that was stupid. What if I'd just wounded him, and he'd fallen down on top of me? He could of eaten me up! I killed him, happened to hit him in the head, but you don't always kill a bear with one shot. I've shot em four, five times and they keep on coming. Finally after I'd convinced that colored fellow that the bear was dead, he come in there and helped me. And we got him out. Bout that time the dog went over there and got after another one, and I told him just go right ahead, I had all the bear I wanted."

I kept scanning the Swamp on both sides of Corapeake Ditch as we drove slowly along, certain now that any minute we were bound to spot another black bear. I never saw another one, though, not that day or any other. I asked Reggie:

"You think they'll learn anything from this bear study—

"Not a damn thing."

"—that people don't already know?"

"I mean, nothing that *I* don't already know."

‽

Reggie and I clambered down the peat and mud wall of the Feeder Ditch and into the trough itself. Where John Foley and I had paddled into and out from Lake Drummond so many years before there stood now no more than ten inches of water. The Feeder, like the Canal it served, was unnavigable and all but dry. We stomped about the muddy beach for a few minutes, collecting a few gigantic oystershells, big bivalves from an era long gone by. Many of them were larger than Reggie's size-eleven shoes, and he kept shaking his head and saying:

"Can you imagine sitting down to a bushel of oysters like *that?*"

It was getting towards suppertime, and we turned south and went on back down Laurel Ditch, passing one place with a number of trees down here and there. "Beavers," Reggie said. "I thought somebody'd been back up here with a chainsaw, but you look—it's beavers!" Beavers in some quarters get heavy credit for clogging and bogging up the Northwest and Nansemond Rivers, setting the processes of peat formation in motion and thereby creating the Great Dismal. If they did once flourish here, beavers have escaped the attention and note of Swamp denizens, visitors, and serious observers since the mid-eighteenth century. But here they were again.

As we got back into North Carolina, Reggie recalled the hunting camp he kept there on the Corapeake Road for about ten years. "I had two old school buses, and we converted one into a kitchen to cook in, the other for beds to sleep in nights, beds for about ten or twelve. We come in one night to cook supper, and our lights was kind of dim and a mouse had got into the lard bucket. And in dipping up the lard to put into the frying pan, the fellow in there cooking, he was about drunk, got the mouse in there and cooked him. And I was the one that reached in to get my sausage and got the mouse. He was all cooked right nice and brown, but I discovered it was a mouse. And I told the other fellows what I had, and they immediately lost what they had already eat. That just about broke up our supper. Fourteen miles back there in the woods, and all we had was kerosene lamps for light, couldn't see too good. After we cooked the mouse, we started cooking then in daytime. Oh, we had a good time. Weekends, holidays, Thanksgiving. Back there outen everybody's way. We had a good time."

Across a brambly burn on Forest Line, the sun was dropping into the cedar spires beyond, and we slowed to admire the juniper thicket again. Reggie fell silent for awhile as we rode, and he sat quietly as I took pictures of two deer on Cross Canal that slowly, but brazenly, approached my car once I had parked it. Now it was late, and in the dim gloaming of the Swamp it felt even later than it was. We were almost back to the airstrip and out of the Swamp before Reggie really spoke again.

"Your granddaddy told me to buy that property, begged me to, but I didn't. He told me it'd make me a fortune, and he told me the truth. But I didn't have any money. Guess I could of gotten it.

"Boy, there was a juniper thicket back there, that if I had a raccoon in my coat, one on each side, I'd of had to turn sideways to get between em. They measured anywhere from eighteen inches to three foot in diameter, and a hundred foot tall. Greatest thing I ever saw, I can't even describe it to you. It was several hundred acres that Roper Lumber Company had *missed*—didn't have airplanes at that time to scout it—and they thought they'd cut everything out, they were selling off their lands, closing down. I come across it while I was out working my traplines, and I told Mose White about it and he asked me, said, 'Would you carry me back and show it to me?' So he came back, took a look, and then he went to the Roper president, the two of em were good friends, and he bought that section from them. Some of the prettiest timber you ever saw. I don't think he give much for it. He run a railroad back in there and cut it, brought it out and built a mill up there on 158, on the highway there. He made shingles there, too, out of the smaller stuff, and selling these boards, faster than he could cut it!

"He made his first million right there, one million dollars, and Mose White was poor as me."

☙

The man whose success in the logwoods loomed so large in Reggie Gregory's mind got his first job two years before Reggie was born. Moses White was born in 1900, and he went to work hauling a mailbag for the Suffolk and Carolina Railroad when he was seven years old. He carried the sack from the post office at Canaan to the train and back, and for this he earned three dollars a month.

The Whites had a fifteen-acre, one-mule farm at Parkville, a community about halfway between Elizabeth City and Hertford, on what was then the extreme southern reach of the Great Dismal. He left Parkville and the farm in 1922, put on hip boots, and went into the Cedar Works Swamp, first keeping books and later taking charge of Cedar Works' logging machinery, for a number of years. He was trapped in a timber cabin in the Great Dismal during the three-foot snowfall of 1927. A few years later, cruising timber in the Alligator River swamps south of Albemarle Sound, he and his men were sleeping on blankets on pushed-down cane at Endless Bay when a four-in-the-morning rainstorm and blow awoke them. With the water all around steadily rising and threatening them, they stood in their hip waders and awaited first light, when it stopped at their waists and receded.

"I was pretty strong into it," Moses White said.

On the sideporch of his golden Dutch Colonial home at Morgans Corner we sat, another baking summer day, while his wife brought us pitchers of icewater, and oiltrucks and logtrucks grinding by on the highway out front nearly drowned his low, muffled voice. The broad boards at our feet were heart pine, and they had been there forty-five years. The porch frame was juniper.

Moses White was a slow-moving, medium-built man with cloudy eyes, a man who never once raised his voice as he surveyed his long life in the Swamp, and I strained constantly to understand him.

"You know," he said, "you look like a Simpson."

"Thank you," I said. "I hope so."

"Well, yeah, you do." And then he, too, told of doing business with my grandfather. "I got a thousand acres that he and Jack Watson had owned. I'd hate to tell you what I paid for it."

I didn't ask.

"Yeah, I would certainly hate to say what I paid for that tract of land."

I sipped icewater and still didn't ask.

"Well, I'll tell you," he said, after a long silence. "I paid em two dollars an acre." When I just shook my head and continued to keep quiet, he quickly added, as if I might somehow think he had shorted those long-dead partners, "Why, they hadn't paid but fifty cents an acre for it!"

A millwhistle blew, sang out over the low lands with a huge and throaty voice, and Moses White looked at his watch and said, "Quitting time, four-thirty. You want to go for a ride?"

We drove up towards the Swamp above the upper Pasquotank River, through cornfields and beanfields, and he talked about the community of Horseshoe as we neared it. "Not too many colored people back here, never got a foothold, I guess. Now, that man lives there, he's been married three, four times—can't never get a woman to stay on with him out here. House over there, man lived there all his life, born there, died there, now his son lives there—and he's seventy!"

On Horseshoe Road where the pavement ended and the road turned a right-angle south were several enormous pines with charred trunks. "Man came along here the other night, ran his pickup truck into those pine trees, caught em on fire. Didn't hurt *him*, though." He pointed at the ditch from whose banks the pines shot forth. "I used to bottle that ditch-water and take it home to drink. I knew a man who always led his teams down there to drink, too."

We weren't too very far from Reggie Gregory's farm when we turned around at a Horseshoe cornpatch, a couple of miles perhaps. Moses White said a bear had been coming out of the Swamp lately and feeding in this field at sunset, and if I returned after a while likely I'd see it. He didn't warn me one way or the other about the bear, but he admonished me severely about the big bushes growing thick along the roadside, tall thorny shafts with beautiful white blossoms all aburst on them.

"Prickly ash, devil's walking stick. Pretty to look at, but you sure can't walk through it. There're thorns on it that'll go right through your hand."

In his yard back at Morgans Corner were a number of shade trees, all of which Moses White had set out himself. The most prominent of them was not a cedar or a cypress, or even a pine, but a sugar maple. The old juniper mill that paid for the golden house and the fancy tree sits some miles west, a few yards south of 158 in Gates County, a dark box in Swamp woods so grown up now that the mill's fat black smokestack doesn't even clear the canopy. The second White mill, a big sawmill right at Morgans Corner, is a dismantled ruin just down the road, its broad tin roofs sagging over a few rusty remnants of the timber trade.

"I had that sawmill going for twenty years, and then I sold it to a man," he said, with regret now in the edge of his voice. "I thought he knew what he was doing, but I found out different."

"What?" I said. "What happened?"

"He closed it down and sold it, sold it off piece by piece. That mill's scattered from here on across Kentucky."

And some new man, young and enough in his prime to be strong into it, had bought most of the boggy woods from Morgans Corner stretching south and west to Parkville, bought twenty-two thousand acres and already cleared eighteen thousand of it. The old man, the three-dollar-a-month mailboy who now paid seven thousand dollars a year in taxes, mused bitterly on that and wondered about his own pinelands that he had held and not cut for fifty years and that now stood a hundred feet tall. And he wondered about more than all of that.

"I'm eighty-five years old," he said. "That seem like a long time to you?"

"Yes, sir," I said, "a right good spell."

"Not to me," said Moses White. "I look back across it, and it's nothing, no time at all. Eighty-five years, and it's like a day."

⪦

3

Washington's Entry

> "The Arm of the Dismal which we passed through to
> get to this New land (as it is called) is 3¼ Miles Mea-
> sured little or no timber in it, but veryfull of Reeds and
> excessive rich."—George Washington, October 1763

Much of the dark water that flows into the Great
Dismal runs in from the west, from Cypress
Swamp. There, where the Desert Road bridges it, I
have heard the call of a hairy woodpecker in early February, and seen
the work of a pileated woodpecker on a tupelo gum stump in the
water: gum chips like half dollars, all dug and pocked out by the
pileated, lay about the base of the stump, and on a bright ice collar
around it just above the water.

Stopping there again on a balmy late April day, I saw poison ivy on
the gum stump where resurrection fern had been growing before. A
great blue heron flew through the tupelos, over and above the trash
that protruded from the swampwaters now that spring had lowered
their level. Here was a brown spaceheater, an old swing set, a faded
red slide-up-the-slots drink box.

Miles to the south, not ten feet below the Virginia line, I took off
into the Swamp on the Corapeake Ditch, down the scarp and past
another skeletal mill-ruin, then south along Sherrill Ditch to Cross
Canal, the ancient twelve-mile ditch that runs the width of the
Swamp from east to west. Cross Canal, also known as Hamburg
Ditch, is the other great bringer of surface water into the Swamp.
But unlike Cypress Swamp, which replenishes Lake Drummond,
Cross Canal drains its water on through the Swamp and into Pas-
quotank River.

This April day, the Cross Canal was flowing right well to the east,
towards the Pasquotank and the main Canal, and, as I backtracked

Tupelo gum brake, Cypress Creek at Desert Road, March 1975

towards the western edge of the Great Dismal and walked over Cross Canal on a wooden footbridge, I watched the waters just pouring into it through rafts of lilypads. A pair of wood ducks jumped up, winged their way back and forth along Cross Canal and the heavy-grassed road beside it, and a yellow-bottomed, brown-winged singer, a prothonotary warbler, flitted quickly in and out of the woods wall. Anxious and at a half trot, for the days fade early in the darkness of tall timber, I stalked rapidly right out of the Swamp and into a plowed field and way overshot my mark:

Remnant Marsh.

These sixty acres of grasses and sedges, of cattails and golden club, were all that remained of Washington's Rice Farm. George Washington had seen Norfleet's mill and meadows here at this mouth of Swamp during his first horseback circumnavigation of the Great Dismal, in May of 1763, and had bought into eleven hundred acres of it three years later. Already men were laboring for his

"Adventurers for Draining the Dismal Swamp," living at Dismal Town near what is now the western end of Washington Ditch and cutting that ditch itself along a causeway into Lake Drummond. Three hundred acres of ditched and diked marsh at Norfleet's, down in Carolina, would help feed them.

I turned around at the Holly Grove field and retraced my steps. Blackberry blossoms were coming on in roadside brambles, and there were stalky lavender flowers and violets growing low. Now the sun had sunk down enough that its last light was coming at a long low slant into the marsh clearing—some seventy-five yards north of Cross Canal through a thick, mature stand of gum and cypress— and making the little green marsh glow like gold.

Into the damp cypress bog I threw myself, for I was determined to walk about the Marsh. My two companions stayed behind at Cross Canal and made me owl-hoot back to them constantly so I wouldn't get lost. No water stood in the Marsh, and there were winding through the thick grass the trails of deer and smaller animals. Young maples and gums had taken hold, and it was clear the whole of the Marsh could soon disappear.

What I saw was not what Washington had in mind when he established the Rice Farm here, but there was nothing else like it in the Swamp today, and I thought it one of the loveliest spots in all of the Great Dismal.

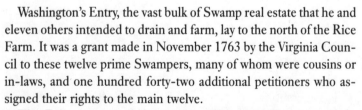

Washington's Entry, the vast bulk of Swamp real estate that he and eleven others intended to drain and farm, lay to the north of the Rice Farm. It was a grant made in November 1763 by the Virginia Council to these twelve prime Swampers, many of whom were cousins or in-laws, and one hundred forty-two additional petitioners who assigned their rights to the main twelve.

The Entry comprised the entire northwestern Swamp, took in everything west of Lake Drummond and due south of it to the Carolina and Virginia line, and very nearly surrounded the Lake

George Washington at Lake Drummond, from Washington Irving's Life of Washington, *1859*

itself. The tract, surveyed originally in 1763 by Gershom Nimmo in four blocks and more conclusively in 1783, was also called the Nelson Grant, after Council-member and venture-partner William Nelson, whose name headed the petition, and it was enormous: forty thousand acres, over sixty square miles. Eleven surveys and a hundred and eighty-nine years later, the great Washington's Entry had proven to be even greater, its final reckoning set at 46,464 acres, over seventy square miles.

The Adventurers assessed themselves five slaves and fifty pounds each in late 1763, and George Washington—armed not only with the Council Grant, but now empowered by the Virginia Assembly with eminent domain rights to cut ditches and roads through adjoining lands—went into the Great Dismal in early summer, 1764, there with the helping hand of his brother John to let tillage begin. Until 1768, when John Washington succeeded him as manager, the future general and president kept the records and ran the business for his fellow Adventurers, even by extra assessment of twelve pounds fining one of them—Virginia House of Burgesses Speaker John Robinson—for sending slaves not up to the task of subjugating the Swamp.

There was farming at Mills Riddick's Dismal Plantation, a roughly triangular tract of two hundred and thirty acres adjoining the Entry at the western end of Washington Ditch, which the Adventurers leased, and then bought in the middle 1760s. Though little or none of the Entry ever felt a hoeblade or plowshare, between Skeeter Field at Dismal Plantation and the Rice Farm down at Norfleet's in Carolina, Washington's crowd for many years tried mightily to make Great Dismal agriculture come to pass.

In 1776 John Washington sent a fifty-five-barrel rice shipment to Antigua, but eleven years later the Adventurers—now known as the Dismal Swamp Company—were still short a hundred and one pounds on a two-hundred-ten-pound sale. The Revolution, though, was harder on the Company than collecting on exports. Several slaves ran off at the War's outset to gain freedom in Virginia Crown Governor Lord Dunmore's Loyalist "Ethiopian" regiment at Norfolk. A British raiding party came down from Portsmouth and attacked Dismal Plantation in 1781, ruining houses and barns and stealing corn, tools, stock, and slaves. The work force had dropped from fifty in 1775 to eleven men, six women, and three children after the raid. Neighbors refused to return runaway slaves, and the hands on the plows in the fall of 1784 were those of Negro girls.

In 1785 the labor situation recaptured George Washington's interest in the Swamp. What of importing Germans to do the work? he asked a Dutch merchant in Alexandria. He inquired in Philadelphia, in Amsterdam, sought Hollanders and Palatines through a factor in Boston. Again, in 1787, he wondered in correspondence with a man named Lutterloh if the Company might settle a hundred German families in the Great Dismal.

None of it worked, and the farm was falling apart. The 1786 crops drowned, leaving the Company with only six casks of rice. They made a three-thousand-pound rice crop in 1787, seven thousand pounds in 1788, but only four barrels in 1789. Half the prior two years' rice, though, was still on hand and unsold.

George Washington never lost faith in the Swamp as farmland,

Corn planters on new land, Arbuckle tract, eastern Dismal, May 1921

though it failed to enrich him at all. In 1793, when the first President tried to sell his interest in the Company to Virginia Governor Light-Horse Harry Lee for five thousand pounds, he bragged to Lee of the Dismal's fabulous soil fertility and its ease of drainage, and put it on a par with "the richest riceland of So. Carolina."

On it went, into the 1800s. The Company ordered Thomas Swepson in 1801 to cut another canal, starting where Washington Ditch emptied into Lake Drummond and running ten miles north by northwest from that juncture all the way out of the Swamp and into the Nansemond River just east of Suffolk. Jericho Ditch was dug around 1810, and the double-duty mill, for sawing lumber and grinding corn, that Swepson built on this new canal was in disrepair by 1812, fixed in 1814, washed out in 1815, and for sale twice with no takers by 1817. New Jericho Mill gates flooded out the Ports-mouth-to-Norfolk highway, and the Nansemond County Court forced the Company to help that county bridge the waters. Jericho Mill did grind for hire all of thirty-six barrels and three pecks of corn in the first half of 1820, but the Company was out of farming and buying grain meal for its workers by 1830.

Surveyor J. H. Reid went about Dismal Plantation counting rings on the stumps when the timber that had grown up there was cut in 1945. Some of the trees were a hundred and fifty years old, and Reid could easily see the old cornrows. Skeeter Field was abandoned before George Washington had even died.

⪽

Shingles, slim slabs of juniper and cypress for roofs and building sides, were the real crop of the Great Dismal, and had been almost from the beginning of Washington's agricultural adventure here.

In 1773 the Company made its first sale: eight thousand twenty-one-inch shingles went for six pounds sterling. By the late 1780s, schooners in Suffolk took on Swamp shingles and sailed them to markets in Philadelphia and New York. In 1795 Company hands and contractors between them cut well over a million and a half shingles.

Shinglegetters worked the easily riven juniper and cypress up into two- and three-foot planks, and cartboys loaded them onto tall two-wheel, one-mule wagons in the remote Swamp shingleyards. Over split-rail tracks laid on corduroy roadbedding came the carts, from the yards to the sides of the Jericho Ditch, where the shingles were transferred to lighters—shallow-draft, flat-bottomed boats bound up Jericho for Suffolk and the Nansemond River.

By 1810, on the strength of shingles, the Dismal Swamp Land Company started paying its first dividends. For most of the next fifteen years, the Company averaged twelve hundred dollars a share, and then eleven hundred a share from 1825 till 1853. It was costing four dollars to rive out a thousand shingles that would sell for twenty dollars. In 1816 there were forty workers employed, the next spring a hundred. From then until the Civil War, the Company sold a million and a half shingles a year, with three-foot juniper shingles as high as thirty dollars a thousand on the New York market in late 1847.

Who were the men who felled the big timber and drew the froes so the Company could pay dividends to an ever-increasing army of assigns and heirs holding fractional shares (like the Society of Shak-

Porte Crayon's Carting Shingles, *1856*

ers, of Pleasant Hill, Ohio, receiving $46.15 in 1831 for its thirteenth of a quarter share willed it by William S. Byrd)? Hired slaves, mostly, though historian John Hope Franklin found that "a considerable number of free Negroes secured work in the Great Dismal Swamp."

In November 1836 the Dismal Swamp Land Company boated an important agricultural reformer down Jericho Ditch through the shingle woods to Lake Drummond. *Farmers' Register* editor Edmund Ruffin, the man who would pull the cannon-lanyard and fire the first shot at Fort Sumter and who would upon Lee's surrender at Appomattox put the muzzle of a silver-mounted shotgun in his mouth and pull the trigger with a forked stick, also took note of the shinglegetters' Swamp life:

"Their houses or shanties," he wrote in the *Register*, "are barely wide enough for five or six men to be in, closely packed side by side—their heads to the back wall and their feet stretched to the open front, close by a fire kept through the night. The roof is sloping, to shed the rain and where highest, not above four feet from the floor. Of the shavings made in smoothing the shingles, the thinnest make a bed for the laborers, and the balance form the only dry and solid foundation for their house, and their homestead or working yard. Yet they live plentifully, and are pleased with their employment—and the main objection to it with their masters (they being generally slaves) and the community, is that the laborers have too much leisure time, and of course spend it improperly. Their heavy labors for the week are generally finished in five, and often in four days—and then the remainder of the week is spent out of the swamp, and given to idleness, and by many to drunkenness. All the work is done by tasks: and the employers have nothing to do except to pay for the labor executed. About 500 men are thus employed in the whole swamp, by the Land Company, and by numerous individual land owners. With all their exposure, the laborers are remarkably healthy, and almost entirely free from the autumnal fevers that so severely scourge all the surrounding country."

These black Swampers called the loose peat soil "sponge," said Sir Charles Lyell after a Dismal visit in late 1841. A progressive English geologist whose work supported Darwin's, Lyell reported that "in the black mire" lay a large forest of unrotted windfalls, which the sawyers mined. "Much of the timber is obtained by sounding a foot or two below the surface and it is sawn into planks while half under water."

Frederick Law Olmsted, the journalist and landscape architect who later designed and built Manhattan's Central Park, toured the Great Dismal in the spring of 1853 and studied the slavehands shingling there. They were rented out by their owners at a hundred dollars a year to work on a task or piecework basis back in the Swamp. Whatever they made beyond the rent on themselves and the cost of their food and clothing, they kept, and Olmsted observed of their considerable freedom:

"The slave is not in the meantime *driven* at all; no force is used to make him 'work smart.' He lives as a free man; having the liberty of the swamp; hunts 'coons, fishes, eats, drinks, smokes, sleeps, and works according to his own will."

Once Edmund Ruffin fired on Fort Sumter and the War was on, the Dismal Swamp Land Company suspended its activity in the Swamp. Most of the mules went to the Confederacy, and a lot that was left got lost in the War. Company Agent Willis Riddick ticked off the losses in a May 1865 letter to the Company's president and managers:

8 light creek lighters	$1,200
10 skiffs	750
8 lake lighters	1,000
26 lighter sides	312
160,000 shingles	1,600
lighter house	100
cribb	150
6 stables and barn	300
200 feet of lumber	36
dwelling house & fixtures	1,500
lot, juniper rails & bolts	600
lot, lumber at Deep Creek	1,000
destruction, country rd. bridge	100
damage to canal	2,000
Total	$10,648

Agent Riddick had had more than the Civil War to deal with. Given the high shingle prices of the late 1840s, it seemed that everyone and his brother from Maine to Florida with access to cypress or juniper had jumped into the roofing and siding business, and there was a glut on the market. After the War there was little demand for cypress shingles, and juniper was running out. In 1853, half the Company's shingles were juniper, but in 1869, only one in seven. Three-foot juniper shingles that cost eight dollars a thousand to cut before the War cost fifteen to twenty dollars a thousand afterwards. The Company had a shingle surplus of a million and a third by 1869, the year of the joining of the transcontinental railroad at Promontory Point, Utah, and now Riddick was scrambling to make money for the Company from cross ties and telegraph poles.

And there was always either too much or too little water. In August 1860 Agent Riddick reported: "We are over run with water, which has been nearly the case all year." When the Swamp was full of water, it was impossible to cut shingles or to get them hauled over submerged corduroy mat roads to drowned ditches. In 1866, supposed to be the driest season in years, shingle lightering stopped. There were bad fires during that July and August, but from then for two years, wrote Riddick, "Wet weather kept most of the lumber in the Swamp." While the shingle surplus built up, the Company's New York broker told Riddick that slate and tin were displacing shingles as roofing material.

The Dismal Swamp Land Company fired Riddick, hired a man named Weston who quickly died, then leased its entire Swamp— Washington's Entry and the several small tracts it had picked up during the past hundred years—to Baird, Roper and Company in April 1871, with several stipulations: a) $12,000 a year, for five years, taxes to be paid by Roper; b) a maximum of one hundred workers at a time; c) nothing under eight inches in diameter to be cut; d) operations on Roper land to continue as well; e) no sublease; f) no machinery (a clause doubtlessly inserted, historian Peter Stewart supposed, out of dread and respect for Roper's power-shaver that, as one Swamp steamboatman marveled, produced "A shingle a clip!"); and, g) Roper was to keep Jericho Ditch clean and clear. Roper held onto the Land Company tract for a good long time—it was still under lease to him in 1888.

But it was a man named William Nelson Camp who bought the Land Company's Swamp, four hundred million board feet of stumpage, in 1899 for $76,500. And with the Camps, a new age now began.

⚞

The first thing William Camp did was to sue the Lake Drummond Canal and Water Company—successor to the Dismal Swamp

Canal Company and rebuilder, in the 1890s, of the main Canal—in an effort to keep that company from drawing down Lake Drummond so far that it dried out Camp's Land Company lands and, in particular, made Jericho Ditch unnavigable. That failed on appeal in 1908, and a year later Camp deeded Washington's Entry and the other lands over to the family timber enterprise in Franklin, Virginia—the Camp Manufacturing Company.

In 1918 lumbering began again in Washington's Entry, this time in the southern area between Lake Drummond and the Carolina line, and from the Richmond Cedar Works line (nowadays Western Boundary Ditch) almost to the western line of the Entry. This was the third cutting in this part of the forest: the Dismal Swamp Land Company had worked it before 1800, Roper had been in there during its leasehold, and now the Jordan Brothers out of Norfolk would cut juniper and hardwood for nine years.

The Camps first went to work at the northern end of their Swamp, in a pine stand between the Norfolk and Western Railroad and the Seaboard Air Line Railroad, and this work not till around 1925. They took on the Swamp in earnest in 1934, when in late April surveyor and lumber cruiser Jack Reid shot the lines for the Dismal Swamp Railroad in from a point on the White Marsh Road about a mile south of Suffolk to a point beyond Jericho Ditch.

Out by the road, at what is now the head of Jericho Lane, was the first Camp No. 7, and there the little timbercutters' town stayed for about three years. Then in July 1937, Reid started putting another rail-line into the Swamp from the Desert Road near Cypress Chapel —what is now Railroad Ditch—and Camp No. 7 moved south to this new railhead in early 1938. Men named Edwards and Smith and Best, in turn, led the Camp hardwood cutting in Washington's Entry, and a man named Hudnell meanwhile cut the juniper.

There was a new generation of Camps coming up into the family business. John M. Camp—William N. Camp's nephew—was running the lumber section around Franklin, and the Great Dismal was within his purview. He loved it, was fascinated by it, and he went into it often, not only to oversee, but to think. Grabbing his hat and bounding off for the morass unexpectedly, he would call back to his wife, "Miss Jones, I'm going to the Swamp." His father, Paul Camp,

Loading logs, Arbuckle tract, eastern Dismal, about 1920

had once brought a bear cub, orphaned when the sawyers cut into its den in a huge hollowed cypress and then killed its mother, home to his daughters to raise as a pet. John Camp would take his son—John, Jr., Jack, who would succeed him running the mill and the lumber business—into the Swamp and let him drive the Dismal Swamp Railroad.

"The Johnson bar," said Mister Jack Camp one gray December morning in Franklin, "is the main lever that you move back and forth that puts the train in gear. This is a great big thing, and when a child got big enough that he could move the Johnson bar from forward to reverse, he was really *somebody*. In the meantime they'd let us pull the bellcord or the whistlecord. I have two of the old bells from the last two steam locomotives, one of them's in the backyard. Beautiful bell, inch and a quarter thick, and when we ring that bell, you can hear it all over the place."

We sat in Jack Camp's den, a small book-lined room paneled in black cypress that came out of the long-drowned Santee Swamp in

Main Train Line in the Dismal, early twentieth century

South Carolina—John Camp had saved enough for each of his three children to have a study of Santee cypress. On the walls were paintings of horses with bobtails, on the coffee table a stuffed puffin from Iceland. The bay window looked out on a long driveway from the white-brick house out to the lane, through an avenue of short oaks and pines, and there was a pineapple-sculpted hollybush with red berries on either side of the walk up to the house.

"The railroads were all put in there on matting," he said, "or on pilings—and we had a lot of wrecks on them because the footing in the Swamp was so treacherous."

"From trains going too fast?" I asked.

"No, just the unevenness of the track, and it would change from day to day, so it was a pretty hazardous kind of operation. Norman T. Poarch was the logging superintendent after Mister E. P. Widmer died, and he was in charge of these railroads. I have been down there when he had train wrecks. Mister Poarch had a horrible temper. And he used to rare and pitch—it's pretty impressive to see a crew of men making a jury-rig crane when you don't have a big railroad crane, to jury-rig some poles or something to get a whole locomotive back on the track. When that locomotive stops the whole operation stops. I enjoyed watching those things go. The crew was all so tolerant of him, he'd just go wild! He was sort of a choleric individual anyway—he would just turn purple until he got that thing back on the track. It's primitive, but they did it."

In the mornings, Jack Camp recalled, the timbercutters, huge black men mostly, would walk up and appear at the Swamp rail-line, and someone driving a Model A or Model T Ford with railroad wheels on it would stop for them and carry them into the woods for the day.

"I remember the beauty of a little tin pot that would probably hold a quart, and they would start out with whatever little meat they were going to have with their lunch, usually piled on top of the rice that was inevitable in these little pots, and it had all been seasoned and it had a little lid on it, shallow. They'd take those pots out there and when they first got there, to the skidder—the man had been up since about three o'clock in the morning getting up steam on that, you know. They would put three tin cans down and put these little pots there and put some coals under it, or put it near the fire box, their tin buckets. And by noon they had beautiful seasoned rice, each grain was standing apart, and they had a hot lunch. And they'd take an hour for lunch and rest."

Camp Manufacturing employed a practice called full-circle logging in the Swamp. From the top of one trimmed-up mast tree cables went out into the woods every ten degrees like wheelspokes, a canvasless bigtop with trees dragged and flown into the center on these thirty-six lines. "At the foot of the mast is where you had your skidder, where you would cut these logs up, and a jump-back loader would come under the skidder operation, load a load of logs and then pull the loaded group back under the skidder to load the next one, and then finally a little steam locomotive would come in there and pick them up," said Jack Camp.

The men who worked this circus in Washington's Entry were so huge, he said, the company stores had to stock especially large sizes of overalls and boots for them. These men, and not infrequently their families, lived in company-built eight-by-sixteen-foot camps sometimes clustered in twos and threes to make houses of them.

Loggers on Arbuckle's big timber train, eastern Dismal, about 1920

This, then, was a log-camp: company store, machine shop, camp houses.

"Depression-style wages, so it was really rough going for the families. And they didn't pay off in money, they paid off in store checks, fiat money, it had serrated edges. You'd come in, pay-day, they'd pay you off in company checks and you'd come back and spend them at the store."

Here in these woodchip outposts of progress and industry and society, the big men and their women and their children would gather and hang around. At least one man had standards for how to behave in a company store, and no shortage of ingenuity about making them stick. "Norman Poarch used to be store manager before he got to be logging manager," Jack Camp said. "He would get upset with the people who would come in and sit on the counter in his store. And he'd rant at em and rant at em, and get em all off of there and five minutes later they'd be back. And he decided that he'd clear that matter up, so he took some wire and stapled some wire to the counter, running three or four inches apart, and then hooked up the ends of that to a Hot Shot battery, the old kind that you used to use in a telephone system and when you'd crank it it would put out a lot of volts that would just shock the bejabbers out of you. And he'd clear that counter in nothing flat when he saw people sitting up there. He seldom had to hit the fellow the second time with that electric charge, he was just off that counter in a hurry!"

⟫

In early summer, 1930, men timbering in Roper Lumber Company woods strayed over and cut a million feet off forty or fifty acres of Camp lands, a bit above where Camp Ditch and East Ditch meet. Seventeen years later a man named Armstrong, cutting for Roper Lumber, put a rail-line up into the extreme southwestern corner of the old Entry and cut half a million feet of hardwoods.

The Camps collected both times.

These timber incursions were apparently accidental, but it had long been otherwise. "They have a pretty deal of Lumber," Virginian William Byrd II observed in Norfolk in 1728, "from the Borderers on the Dismal, who make bold with the King's Land there abouts, without the least Ceremony. They not only maintain their Stocks upon it, but get Boards, Shingles and other Lumber out of it in great Abundance."

Much later, even though the Virginia legislature in 1779 exempted the Dismal Swamp Land Company from a law voiding all unsurveyed land entries, people were staking claims on Washington's Entry, and the Company treasurer panicked. "The opinion prevails," David Jameson wrote to Adventurer Dr. Thomas Walker in 1783, "that they will hold them as we have not proved to survey." Even with a new survey of the forty thousand acres registered the next year, there would still and always be trouble.

In the 1790s the Company's agent told the manager that people were trespassing on Washington's Entry and raiding Company timber because they did not believe the Company grant was legal. The high sheriffs of both Norfolk and Nansemond Counties agreed with the raiders. So did Sheperd, the Company's agent.

Between December of 1814 and May of 1816, two shingling partners named Butt and Bartee were supposed to have cut illegally hundreds of thousands of shingles off the Entry. Complaints came in from contractors who bought timber from the Company and then went into the Swamp only to discover raiders at work in that same timber. A century later, Camp surveyor J. R. Kirk went over the entire Washington's Entry because Camp and Richmond Cedar Works were in court in a contest over the Entry's eastern line.

Still, Jack Reid, a slight, wiry man once treed for a whole night in the Swamp by a herd of feral cattle, was wary in his surveyor's summary of the Camps' Swamp holdings, writing in 1952:

"Gentlemen: Since the adjoining timber has all been cut and lines all set up and well marked with monuments, I do not think you will have any more law suits, however . . . these maps and notes might be worth something to a surveyor in the future as an indication of what he needs to look for in case of trouble."

"I know we had a lot of controversy about it," Jack Camp said to me that December day in his den. "Because it was ringed by people who were all pretty damn independent. When we tried to get the hunting established so that we would have everything organized in hunting clubs who in turn would be responsible for fire control in a measure, our attorney got in touch with one man who said, 'Look, don't bother me about hunting. I hunted here, and my father and my sons, and we're gon hunt here as long as we want to hunt here. You can forget trying to tell us what not to do.' Now that's how rugged a lot of the people were around the edge of the Swamp. If people got upset with you, they'd set your woods on fire. That was their retaliation, you couldn't catch em. They had all kinds of devices that would allow them to be out of the woods before the fire ever was detected.

"We're a very litigious society now and 'Hey, what can we get them for?' People in the Swamp are even more so. You're either for us or against us. Boy, once they get something against you, they'll burn your woods, or shoot you, or something like that. Pretty tough crowd."

🦫

One year in the middle of January, just after Jack Camp got out of the service in World War II, he spent a week in the Great Dismal with a surveying team, eight men in two boats and one canoe. They portaged their craft and nearly half a ton of coal around the Feeder Ditch spillway, then crossed the Lake to settle in for a Swamp spell at Jack's Camp and Little Ennie's Bear Camp. Jack Camp sat facing astern, and when they reached the far shore he stood and a sheet of ice fell off the back of his coat.

Along with them was the man from New England who had developed the stereopticon photograph technique of cruising, or estimating, standing timber by studying aerial photographs. "Not only count the stems, which is what they call individual trees," Jack Camp explained, "but also estimate the diameter and the height. Set these things up just right, and you could do a timber cruise in your living room." The team that January was in there to check on the ground the accuracy of drawing-board cruises done back in the Camp offices in Franklin. At daylight they would start out, splitting up into several parties going in different directions.

"I never was colder in my life," said the timberman, "because my boots leaked. So by the second day I found out the best way to cure that was to cut holes in em so the water would run out as fast as it ran in."

The Camps had gotten into the paper business in the late 1930s and were pulling out of hardwoods. For most of Jack Camp's tenure in the Camp enterprise, the Great Dismal Swamp was a valuable and unproductive hardwood reserve with great tinderbox potential. So Jack Camp rarely returned to the Swamp after that, once or twice by his own estimation, because it never held for him any of the powerful fascination that gripped his father, and his father's father before him.

"To me," he said, "it didn't have the charm."

Puncheon path along swamp channel between a western tributary and the main Dismal, 1880s

In 1956 Camp Manufacturing merged with Union Bag and became known as Union Camp. Years later, after much tough study and negotiation with The Nature Conservancy, America's premier land-preservation organization, Union Camp donated its Swamp—where red maple now grew rampantly—through the Conservancy to the Department of Interior's Fish and Wildlife Service. Union Camp got a twelve and a half million dollar tax advantage, and unending accolades from shareholders and schoolchildren alike for the largest single land donation to that date ever made the American people for wildlife preservation. Washington's Entry went back to the people on Washington's Birthday, 1973.

It is now called Great Dismal Swamp National Wildlife Refuge, and it has grown in the years since to a size of about one hundred and six thousand acres. No shingles have been cut here in the old Entry, no traincars or truckloads of cypress or gum have come out of it in nearly a generation. No one named Camp now works at Union Camp.

And the last time I tried to make my way west down Cross Canal to the marsh remnant of Washington's Rice Farm, the roadway was all grown up from the ditchbank on one side to the gumswamp on the other in blackberries high as a man's head, and the thick thorny bramble was impenetrable and inaccessible to a man without a blade.

4

Lost in the Desert

"In this desert inaccessible,
Under the shade of melancholy boughs."
—William Shakespeare, *As You Like It*

My Lamborn cousins and I used to play hard in the sandy woods behind their house in Virginia Beach. Sixty-first Street stopped high up on a dune, still on the windward side, and then the dune dropped away on the leeward into a swampy forest that we were always warned was endless.

We spent hours rolling down the dunesides in the thick cardboard moving barrels this Navy family had in abundance, and down in the big woods, in the tall pines and liveoaks and around mysterious shallows, pools, and ponds, we chopped and hacked with the little hatchets and hunting knives our grandparents had given us not long before. We lit fires and put them out, watched the ant-devil bugs hiding in their conical sandy sinks, tramped for hours on deerpaths and jeeptrails, and when we finally came back up the steep and slipping incline and our folks asked us where we'd been we answered all and nothing:

"In the woods."

This was just below Cape Henry, in the eastern range of Fort Story somewhere, and we knew the woods was a very special place, for we never saw anyone else in there but ourselves. We were pioneers in a deserted place, men among men at the age of eight.

The name of our forest wilderness was "The Desert," but we didn't know that. Botanist Thomas Kearney had called this eastern reach of the Great Dismal that in 1901, echoing engineer Benjamin Latrobe, who said in 1799 that the locals called it by that name even then. Nor did we know that the Swamp was also called "The Desert" in Camden and Currituck Counties, in North Carolina, or that there was a Four-Mile Desert Road in the southern part of the Swamp just west of Elizabeth City and a just plain Desert Road running up along the Suffolk Scarp on the Swamp's west side.

And we certainly had no idea that one of the leaders of an elaborate survey commission setting the boundary between Virginia and Carolina—the line my cousins and I would straddle north of Moyock in order to be in two states at one time—had come up against the Dismal in 1728 and called the whole massive morass "this horrible desart."

🐾

That man called himself Steddy, and he was but one of the motley group that gathered at the Atlantic in early March 1728, finally to draw the line. His fellow Virginia boundary commissioners were the two gentlemen Firebrand and Meanwell, and along with them expressly to minister to the heathens of the Carolina frontier was a chaplain, Doctor Humdrum. "The Flower & Cream of the Council of that Province," Steddy remarked of the four Carolina commissioners: Judge Jumble, Shoebrush, Plausible, and Puzzlecause, who, to the eternal credit of themselves and their Old North State, had already by letter shown their gratitude for the preacher who might make "a great many Boundary Christians."

These eight, with their boats and bearers and several surveyors—Astrolabe and Orion for the Virginians, young Bo-otes for the Carolinians—drove a cedar post about two hundred yards up the north shore of Currituck Inlet, a point they reckoned to be 36 degrees 31 minutes north latitude, and headed west. Not before, however, Steddy cavalierly looked down at Carolina across the Inlet and at the first two citizens he saw.

They were "a Marooner who had the Confidence to call himself an Hermit" and "a Female Domestick as wild & dirty as himself. His Diet is chiefly Oysters, which he has just Industry enough to gather from the Neighboring Oyster Banks, while his Concubine makes a Practice of driving up the Neighbour's Cows for the advantage of their milk." His clothing, wrote Steddy, was in the main his beard, and hers too fore and aft were her flowing tresses. "Thus did these Wretches live in a dirty State of Nature, and were mere Adamites, Innocence only excepted."

The border party pressed on. They ran aground in Currituck Sound, waded in the pluff mud of the marshes. Shoebrush broke a tooth on a biscuit and nearly dallied with a black woman in an isolated cabin. Firebrand and several others—but not Steddy, who had retired early—drank and cavorted with a "Tallow-faced Wench" one night at Ballance's Plantation. "They examined all her hidden Charms, and play'd a great many gay Pranks," Steddy reported. "While Firebrand who had the most Curiosity, was ranging over her sweet Person, he pick't off several Scabs as big as Nipples, the Consequence of eating too much Pork."

Two days before the fun at Ballance's, Steddy had already grasped an essential fact of our Carolina character: "The Truth of it is, these People live so much upon Swine's flesh, that it don't only encline them to the Yaws, & consequently to the downfall of their Noses, but makes them extremely hoggish in their Temper, & many of them seem to Grunt rather than Speak in their ordinary conversation."

By the evening of March 13, 1728, the boundary linesmen had come upon the eastern edges of the Great Dismal. The Carolina commissioners had earlier wondered if the best way to shoot the line through the Swamp would be to leave off on the east side, find the same latitude on the west side and proceed from there to Chowan River.

Everyone, excepting the commissioners, wanted to press on through the Swamp, for the immortal glory of it. They drew lots for the honor, whereupon the losers offered the winners money to be allowed to go in their places. Where the Carolinians, Judge Jumble and the rest, had thought the Great Dismal to be thirty miles wide, Steddy wrote that people living on the edge guessed it to be no more than seven or eight miles through. "At the Same time," he noted, "they were Simple enough to amuse our Men with Idle Stories of the Lyons, Panthers and Alligators, they were like to encounter in that dreadful Place."

As they entered the strange land of "Bryars and Gall Bushes," of "Ground moist and trembling under our feet like a Quagmire, insomuch that it was an easy Matter to run a Ten-Foot-Pole up to the Head in it, without exerting any uncommon Strength," one of the chosen got cold feet. This was Orion, one of the Virginia surveyors and a mathematics professor at William and Mary with "so very few Scholars," according to Steddy, "that he might be well enough spared from his post for a short time." Steddy had also noticed straightaway, when the party was just starting out at Currituck Inlet, that Orion seemed quite puzzled by the task of surveying.

Now Orion wished he were back at College. He was afraid the buzzards were going to pick him clean, deep in the Dismal. Next morning, March 14, Orion decided that if he must go, he would take plenty of extra clothes, his Sunday suit, too. Rather, men already bearing eight days' provisions would take it all for him—his extra gear loaded them up to about sixty pounds apiece.

Before the fifteen who were actually going through the Swamp dove in, Steddy at its edge gave them a speech. He preached spirit and constancy, saluted their vigor, told them to pray. "And grant we may meet on the other Side in perfect Health & Safety," he concluded.

"Huzza! Huzza! Huzza!" cheered the Fifteen.

For two hours Steddy and Meanwell and Puzzlecause stayed with the Dismalites, thrashing through the reeds and briars in the spongy mire for about a mile. Then the three commissioners bade the Swampers farewell and went to rejoin Firebrand, Doctor Humdrum, and the rest of the politicians.

The Great Dismal Survey was on.

The men slowly chopped through the brambles and the windfallen, lapped cypress trees, making a mile a day, needing rum more than ever or anywhere else, wrote Steddy, to fight off the Dismal's Bad Water, its Malign Air. Steddy and the others journeyed around the north side of the Swamp, noticing "pretty Girls here as wild as Colts," drinking strong liquors and strong beer.

When he turned in on a pallet of downfeathers, while it rained outside, Steddy was uneasy in the comfort of Captain Meade's on the Nansemond. He felt sorry for "the poor Dismalites." On Saint Patrick's Day, Steddy's group prayed for their "Suffering Friends" in the Swamp, and the next day wound down the western side of the

Dismal, past Cypress Swamp and Corapeake, to the plantation of Thomas Speight. Speight, an associate justice of the General Court of North Carolina, was down with the gout in both knees. He had no word of the surveyors, so the commissioners now ordered guns fired, drums beaten, hoping for some signal from their fellows. The following day, they sent patrols off both north and south of Speight's, to keep blasting away with guns.

The Fifteen for whose ears all that gunfire was intended were at that point only about one-third of their way into the Swamp, and heard nothing that they, or the Great Dismal itself, did not sound off for them. Somehow the men kept their spirits up, all but the peevish Orion, who in trying to pull rank one hot day got well told off by the linesman Robin Hix.

"Hix," Orion said, "I desire you to carry my great-coat."

"No, thank you, my lord," Hix replied to the incompetent surveyor, "for I have already as great a burden as I can stagger under."

They slept on cypress bark, but the water percolated into their bedding anyway. They worked harder by the day, cutting through miles of cedar thicket on reduced rations. They eyed John Evans, the fattest amongst them, and joked with him that he would go first to pot, if it should come to that.

"Dead or alive," he said, "I should be glad to be useful to such worthy good friends."

They started looking hungrily at the survey-party dog. One of them dreamed Indians were fixing to barbecue him.

Away at Speight's, Doctor Humdrum was busy with all the children the countryside had spewed forth for him to christen. Steddy asked Humdrum to record the christenings, "that we might keep an Account of the good we did." Speight's daughter Rachel, whom Steddy had reckoned "a smart Lass" and who was washing out his linens, overheard this and asked:

"Who is to keep an account of the evil?"

"You should be my secretary for that," said Steddy, "if you would go along with me."

On March 21, their eighth day in the Swamp, the Dismalites abandoned the Dividing Line and ran for their lives, striking out due west and covering four miles of cedar swamp by nightfall. They had gone through all their food, but now they could hear cattle lowing and dogs barking, and it gave them heart.

Next morning they saw crows flying above, and set out again, reaching before long a pine swamp with firmer bottom than the wet and rotten peat-muck through which they had been slogging. The pines grew tall in waters knee-deep for nearly a mile. At mid-morning they struck dry land, and came famished out of the Swamp to Peter Brinkley's, near Corapeake. Brinkley was full of curiosity, but the surveyors were too empty and weak for inquisition.

"But pray, Gentlemen," Brinkley said, "answer me One Question at least: what shall we get for your Dinner?"

"No matter what," they said, "provided it be but Enough."

✍

In the story Steddy told, he gave himself the leading role. Steddy, the first journalist of the Great Dismal, was the remarkable William Byrd II, and the rest of the cast to whom he gave so many farce-player names were:

Meanwell	William Dandridge
Firebrand	Richard Fitz-William
Judge Jumble	Christopher Gale
Plausible	Edward Moseley
Shoebrush	John Lovick
Puzzlecause	William Little
Orion	Alexander Irvine
Astrolabe	William Mayo
Bo-otes	Samuel Swann
Doctor Humdrum	Peter Fountain

Virginia and Carolina had been at odds for sixty years over where to draw the line. The 1663 Carolina Charter had declared the boundary between the colonies to be thirty-six degrees, north latitude, but another charter two years after that set the border at thirty-six degrees, thirty minutes. Contentious citizens newly settled in the broad band of land between Lake Drummond on the north and

Albemarle Sound on the south were refusing to pay quitrents to Virginia or to obey Carolina laws about Indian trade or both. There had been several failed boundary attempts before Byrd's party, the most recent one of which, in 1710, fell apart when Carolinians Edward Moseley—Byrd's Plausible—and John Lawson—whom Indians would torture to death on the Neuse River the next year—denounced the Virginians' surveying instruments, a point with which inveterate Virginian Byrd oddly enough agreed years later.

The line Byrd's party pulled through the Great Dismal—the Dismalites having returned to their task fed and freshened—stood one shy of a hundred sixty years. Between November 1887 and March 1888 another Carolina and Virginia team marked the state line through the Swamp. Carolina Commissioner Pruden found the 1728 line "remarkable for its accuracy," and the main contest this time was not between the two states, but between the boundarymen and all God's weather: constant rain from late November to late February, a foot of snow in December, a foot and a half in January, bitter cold, the main Canal and Drummond, too, iced over.

Mapping in the Dismal never got any easier. Engineers working on topographic maps here after World War II found the going slow, though they had the relative luxury of getting in and out of the Swamp aboard a Camp logging train they called the "Juniper Special," or, when they were not riding, the lesser delights of precarious rail-walking and hip-booted ditch striding. Their brush-cutters suffered regular, accidental leg-slashings from the machetes they used, their tripod would sink till the transit was only a couple of feet off the ground and would not stay level, and their base-line across northwest Lake Drummond they pulled by threading a three-hundred-foot steel tape through fish-net corks and floating the strand over the water.

Wiry Jack Reid, the Camps' surveyor, said in 1952 he had run the state line several times from a point just off U.S. 258, west of the Dismal, all the way to Northwest River, east of the Swamp, excepting three miles. "I have never found any two consecutive courses the same." He blamed 1887 survey engineer Harry Greenleaf of Elizabeth City, who "did not survey out the line straight through on the ground," but ran traverses and tried to figure closures instead of seeing if lines from stones he set really tied up on the ground. Of the 1728 work, on the other hand, Reid offered this salute:

"I have also run out the old state line from White Marsh Road to the Northwest River. This survey was exceptionally good and as near as I could tell by retracing with a compass, is straight all the way through and shows that Byrd [*sic*] actually surveyed all of it out on the ground."

William Byrd of Westover was a skillful politician, an acquisitive planter who inherited 26,000 acres and passed on to his heirs 180,000. If he seemed publicly priggish, he was privately no prude: he made love to his wife (gave her "a flourish," he said) on his billiard table; he "rogered" her regularly, an early diary noted. And out on the boundary-line trail years later, at Thomas Speight's, he alleged with wistful humor that had either of Speight's daughters tried to slip into his bed, rather than the boorish Edentonian who really made the attempt, "We shou'd perhaps have made no Words: but in truth the Captain had no Charms that merited so particular an Indulgence."

From his rich and ribald daybook of the 1728 survey, *The Secret History of the Line*, Byrd then created a much different record of the journey, the *History of the Dividing Line betwixt Virginia and North Carolina*, here turning his wit from the sex and squabbling of *The Secret History* to a running denunciation of the unhealthy Carolina heathens—and of the "vast Body of mire and Nastiness," the Great Dismal Swamp. Neither manuscript reached print for generations —Edmund Ruffin published the *History* in 1841, but *The Secret History* did not surface until 1929.

Even so, the manuscripts apparently circulated in Byrd's own time, and his views on what to do with the Great Dismal Swamp— drain it, timber it, raise hemp on it, shoot an Albemarle to Chesapeake canal through it—were well known to influential Virginians during the long period between his death in 1744 and publication. George Washington, whose wife was the niece of Meanwell, or William Dandridge, of the 1728 boundary team, did not just chance upon the Swamp as a likely project for his fourth decade. And Thomas Jefferson, who had read Byrd's journals, responded quite favorably to North Carolina Congressman Hugh Williamson's push for an Albemarle and Chesapeake canal in 1785.

Though Byrd is oft credited with naming the Great Dismal, a man writing a missionary thirteen years before Byrd's boundary referred to a piece of Pasquotank County as "dismal swamp," and lowland Carolinians in those old days used the words "swamp" and "dismal" interchangeably. There is an East Dismal Swamp in the great neck of land between Albemarle Sound and Pamlico River, and a Little Dismal in Johnston County a ways upstate.

The real wonder is not whether he named it, but rather why Byrd wrote so harshly of the Great Dismal, skewing his recorded view to the point he claimed that "neither Bird nor Beast, Insect nor Reptile" could live there. Was this his bold-stroke attempt to get Crown or public monies for drainage and exploitation of the Swamp, by overstating the extent of its dismality and danger? The Swamp, mysterious and unknown and unorganized and unutilized, was a challenge, an affront to Byrd's neoclassical sense of order, its heart and soul the very opposites of his own. George Washington, working with Byrd's second-hand knowledge of the place, would range its dark reaches, would sleep on the shores of Drummond's Pond, would see in the Swamp "a glorious paradise." But Washington was an American, and Byrd had spent half his life in London. At the very start of the survey that nearly lost itself and the lives of fifteen men in the Great Dismal, William Byrd at Currituck Inlet looked eastward past the great breakers and revealed himself:

"I often cast a longing Eye towards England, & Sigh'd."

⤊

Most of those who were ever lost in The Desert wanted to be.

These were the runaway slaves of the eighteenth and nineteenth centuries, a huge population of whom historian Merl Eppse wrote: "The Dismal Swamp Colony of Negroes continued from generation to generation, defying and outwitting the slaveowners right in the midst of the strongest slave-holding communities in the South."

When did this Colony, if it could really be called that, get started?

William Byrd may have seen its beginnings during the boundary-line tour. Camped near Mossy Point on the evening of March 11, 1728, Byrd and Carolinian John Lovick took a walk into the woods and came upon a family of mulattos that Byrd was fairly sure were runaways, and he wrote:

"It is certain many Slaves Shelter themselves in this Obscure Part of the World, nor will any of their righteous Neighbors discover them. On the Contrary, they find their Account in Settling such Fugitives on some out-of-the-way-corner of their Land, to raise Stocks for a mean and inconsiderable Share, well knowing their Condition makes it necessary for them to Submit to any Terms. Nor were these worthy Borderers content to Shelter Runaway Slaves, but Debtors and Criminals have often met with the like Indulgence."

Runaways were early a bitter fact of life for the Dismal Swamp Land Company, in the 1770s and 1780s. By early summer, 1802, a black man named Tom Copper promoted himself as the general who could and would lead a murder rampage against the whites of Pasquotank County. Quickly outlawed, Copper was supposed to have a hideout camp somewhere in the southern Swamp. And, though nothing more than general unrest came of Tom Copper's threat, this prefigured Nat Turner's bloody uprising in Southampton County, Virginia, just thirty miles west of the Swamp, and predated it by twenty-nine years.

In late October 1817, Samuel Huntington Perkins, a young Yale graduate bound for Hyde County, North Carolina, to tutor plantation girls, landed in Norfolk on his way south. He was immediately impressed with the city, and wrote:

"Norfolk is one of the most dissipated places in the Union. At least two thirds of the young men have the venereal disorder, & frequently die with it. So vitiated have they become that a negro will satisfy their wishes, & a yellow wench appears to be their highest ambition. Though the inhabitants looked like walking spectres, they informed me that they considered it the healthiest place in the country."

Having roamed Norfolk for a few hours and passed that summary judgment, the Yankee tutor hired a horse and buggy and set off down the Canalbank road towards Elizabeth City. The forewarnings he had obviously received unsettled him about his journey through the Swamp. "Travelling here without pistols is considered very dangerous," Perkins wrote, "owing to the great number of runaway negroes. They conceal themselves in the woods & swamps by day and frequently plunder by night." By the time he reached Lake Mattamuskeet in mid-November, Perkins had learned that "not long since a woman was discovered in the centre of the Great Dismal Swamp. There she and her six children had lived for years preferring the horrors of such a place and the enjoyment of freedom, to the comforts [of] civilized life when attended with the loss of liberty."

There was no shortage of speculation about how many runaways took to the Dismal. "The Great Swamp is supposed to afford concealment to upwards of a thousand runaway slaves," an anonymous traveler wrote in *Chambers' Edinburgh Journal*, December 1850, "who glean a miserable living within its gloomy recesses, though many are believed to be secretly supplied with food by friends more fortunate in their owners than were the fugitives." Eppse, the historian, guessed the Great Dismal to be the hideout of "over one million and a half dollars worth of slaves."

Aboard a ship returning from Germany in October of 1842, Henry Wadsworth Longfellow penned for his "Poems on Slavery" this hymn to the lone runaway, "The Slave in the Dismal Swamp":

In dark fens of the Dismal Swamp
The hunted Negro lay;
He saw the fire of the midnight camp,
And heard at times a horse's tramp
And a bloodhound's distant bay.

Where will-o'-the-wisps and glow-worms shine,
In bulrush and in brake;
Where waving mosses shroud the pine,
And the cedar grows, and the poisonous vine
Is spotted like the snake;

Where hardly a human foot could pass,
Or a human heart would dare,
On the quaking turf of the green morass
He crouched in the rank and tangled grass,
Like a wild beast in his lair.

A poor old slave, infirm and lame;
Great scars deformed his face;
On his forehead he bore the brand of shame,
And the rags, that hid his mangled frame,
Were the livery of disgrace.

All things above were bright and fair,
All things were glad and free;
Lithe squirrels darted here and there,
And wild birds filled the echoing air
With songs of Liberty!

On him alone was the doom of pain,
From the morning of his birth;
On him alone the curse of Cain
Fell, like a flail on the garnered grain,
And struck him to the earth!

Another Northern writer who never set foot in the Great Dismal but who also took up the runaway theme was Harriet Beecher Stowe, in the novel *Dred, A Tale of the Dismal Swamp*. His character inspired by Southampton slave rebel Nat Turner, Dred in Stowe's fiction is the son of the real Charleston insurrectionist Denmark Vesey, who was betrayed, foiled, and hanged in 1822. From his island in the Swamp, Dred fights the white world, even appearing one night in a tree high above a white people's revival, speaking loftily, Biblically, against the order of the day, against slavocracy. Shot by white hunters, Dred makes it back to his Swamp island to die. Stowe's novel appeared in late summer 1856, four years after the phenomenal success of her *Uncle Tom's Cabin*, and just as the Dred Scott Case—in which a black man who went from slave state Missouri to free Wisconsin territory for four years and then back later sued for his freedom—was ending its ten-year journey to the United

States Supreme Court. *Dred*'s notices were poor, but *Dred*'s author was not. Over three hundred thousand copies circulated in the United States and the United Kingdom within a year, and the writer who drank Catawba wine to see herself through the strain of its composition merely remarked, "Who cares what critics say?"

Apparently for some stretch of antebellum years, according to Swamp literary historian Robert Haywood Morrison, there was "an organized rendezvous for both runaway slaves and white criminals" at Culpeper Island. Sometime before the Civil War a battalion of slaveholders found this high-ground hideout—several hundred acres in extreme northeastern Camden County, two or three miles east of the main Canal and just below the Virginia line—and tore the community apart.

Frederick Law Olmsted during his Southern tour gave a buggy ride to a black man he called Joseph Church, who was the property of a religious congregation. Church liked "minding himself" as a lumberman in the Swamp, he told Olmsted, and he knew much about the runaway life. "Children were born, bred, lived and died here," Olmsted wrote. "Joseph Church told me he had seen skeletons, and had helped to bury bodies recently dead. There were people in the swamps still, he thought, that were the children of runaways, and who had been runaways all their lives." They preyed on the farms and plantations at the Swamp's edges, or, probably more often, hired themselves sub rosa to the slave gangs shingling in the Great Dismal most of the year. A slave shinglegetter's provision needs might shoot up, but just as mysteriously might his output of shingles. He was hiring help from the phantom labor force, another level of exploitation below the lowest, and no one complained.

Olmsted didn't guess how many runaways were in the Great Dismal when he passed through in 1853, but he thought the population must be way down after years of dog-drivers—slavehunters with hounds—on the runaways' trails. "Blood-hounds, fox-hounds, bull-dogs, and curs were used. . . . I have since seen a pack of negro-dogs, chained in couples, and probably going to the field. They were all of a breed, and in appearance between a Scotch stag-hound and a fox-hound."

"Oh, yes," Joseph Church answered Olmsted when he asked if

Porte Crayon's Horse Camp, *Jericho Ditch, 1856*

the hunters ever shot runaways. "But some on 'em would rather be shot than be took, sir." It was easy, he said, for the drivers to tell a runaway from a legally rented-out slave shingler.

"How do they know them?" Olmsted asked.

"Oh, dey looks *strange*."

"How do you mean?"

"*Skeared* like, you know, sir, and kind o' strange, cause dey hasn't much to eat, and ain't decent like we is."

Three years later, on his way back up Jericho Ditch from Lake Drummond, the witty, romantic author and illustrator Porte Crayon—David Hunter Strother of Winchester, Virginia—risked his life for a brief glimpse of a runaway slave. Crayon's covered barge stopped at "Horse Camp, the head-quarters of the shingle-makers in this district," for refueling—the two men trudging the ditchside towpath, leaning into fore-and-aft poles and pushing the boat bearing Crayon up Jericho, wanted dinner.

Crayon took the moment to explore. Horse Camp was an amalgam of slab-topped, open-sided pole sheds, with a great store of "bacon, salt fish, meal, molasses, whisky, and sweet potatoes, be-

Osman

sides plenty of fodder for the mules." While he sketched the camp, in from the Swamp's interior rumbled seven high-piled shingle carts, two-wheeled wagons commanded by black drovers and drawn by mules over the corduroy log causeway.

"I had long nurtured a wish to see one of those sable outlaws who dwell in the fastnesses of the Swamp," wrote Crayon, who then struck out alone along the causeway. "When I had gone a mile or more I heard the sounds of labor, and saw the smoke from a camp-fire." Crayon stepped off the causeway and into the Swamp, thrashing about in the underbrush until he heard someone else nearby. "I paused, held my breath, and sunk quietly down among the reeds.

"About thirty paces from me I saw a gigantic negro, with a tattered blanket wrapped about his shoulders, and a gun in his hand. His head was bare, and he had little other clothing than a pair of ragged breeches and boots. His hair and beard were tipped with gray, and his purely African features were cast in a mould betokening, in the highest degree, strength and energy. The expression of the face was of mingled fear and ferocity, and every movement betrayed a life of habitual caution and watchfulness. He reached forward his iron hand to clear away the briery screen that half concealed him while it interrupted his scrutinizing glance. Fortunately he did not discover me, but presently turned and disappeared."

Crayon waited, then bolted for the causeway, where he made a quick sketch "of the remarkable figure." At dinner back in Horse Camp he put the sketch where his bargemen would surely see it. "As Jim Pierce passed it he uttered an exclamation, and beckoned to Ely. I fancied I heard the word Osman.

" 'Do you know that, Jim?'

" 'No, Sir,' said he, promptly; 'dunno nothin' bout um.' "

How many Osmans there must have been, how many women and children living in the horror of desperation in clawed-out camps, in lightning-burnt patches. Surely a few of them managed a little Swamp society, like those at the rogues' harbor of Culpeper Island, but any notion of reconstructed African villages springing up whole and happy in the Great Dismal before the War—the dreamy vision of a recent scholar—seems fantasy run away. Many of those hundreds who fled one wretchedness for another could doubtless have

Suffolk end of Jericho Ditch, 1880s

echoed the former fugitive who spoke with sportsman Alexander Hunter in Suffolk right after the Civil War:

"I was in the Swamp nineteen years," he said, "and never seen a woman. I had plenty of whiskey and tobacco, but what I longed for was a real old plantation cornshucking."

🌿

In modern times, since the Civil War, many others have gotten lost in the Great Dismal, lost to the world if not themselves. During one of his late-nineteenth-century explorations of the Swamp, Alexander Hunter came across two families living in a one-room cabin "across the lake," and gave this census enumeration:

"Five women, one boy, sixteen children—of all sizes and colors, thirteen sucking pigs, five dogs, ten puppies, four cats (three tabbies and a tom), two litters of kittens, five dissipated-looking ducks, three hens, a melancholy-looking rooster, one sociable sow, and ninety million mosquitoes."

Around 1910 there was apparently an Italian living somewhere in the Swamp's north end—the Italian consul to Norfolk paid the hermit immigrant a call. My friend, the oldtime trapper Reggie Gregory, remembers from his boyhood two old men—his cousin Mark Temple and another man named Mitt Rhodes—living in a camp on one of the eight or so camel-ridges that run east and west in the lower part of the Swamp, supposedly there in the hire of Richmond Cedar Works to live there long enough that Cedar Works might acquire their stretch of Swamp by squatter's rights. And he knew of another hill a mile deep in the Swamp east of Pasquotank River, Stanley's Hill, where a man named Stanley lived and farmed. "The old walnut tree and part of the old chimbley are still back there, and the signs of the corn rows are still there today."

As far as anyone getting lost—dead lost—Reggie only knew of one man who went into the Great Dismal and never returned, a black man who everyone supposed froze to death. "He's still back there, far as I know. We looked for him, but didn't never find him. He had a little dog with him, and the dog come to us. Got the dog, but didn't never find him."

Reggie was in on a search for an Army plane that fell into the Swamp, twenty years or so ago. It was cold and rainy, and a search plane spotted the downed aircraft, flew over, and dropped Reggie a map showing where the plane was. He gathered a bunch of men, including some Coast Guardsmen, borrowed Moses White's dinky-train engine, and pulled a boxcar with the seekers in it up into the Swamp. They went as far as they could on the train, then walked up an old switch, its rails taken up but its cross ties still there, about a mile, and called and called for the pilot in the night, but there was no answer and they took him for dead.

Next day Reggie's search party returned to the same place, and this time the pilot answered their calls. He had been asleep under the wing the night before, he said, and hadn't heard them. "He had landed in a juniper thicket, just went right in that thicket and just bent them right over, broke em off and landed down like that. Tore the plane all to pieces, and he wasn't hurt. That's all that saved him, those thick treetops. That plane was high as that wall from the ground," Reggie said, pointing to an eight-foot shedside of his barn. "It never come to the ground."

"Was it a big plane?" I asked him.

"Yeah, it had a straight engine into it, that motor was long as from here to that post. Looked like about sixteen cylinders in it. Some of the boys got the wheels off of it and brought em home. I think they still got em."

≈

About 1950 a couple of boys in their early teens rambled down Jericho Ditch towards Lake Drummond, then wandered off into the Swamp in the area below the Jericho firetower and to the north and east of the ditch itself. Where they were, the Jericho Ditch flattened out and was indiscernible from the rest of the great woods. Since they could not find the ditch, they had no route out. After hearing from a distressed and frightened mother that night, the Nansemond game warden went down Jericho as far as he could in a boat, lying down in the boat and sliding under the dense and low-hanging foliage. The warden hollered, fired a gun, but the boys never heard any of it.

In the morning the warden had a cub plane fly the length of Jericho Ditch, back and forth from Five Points at the north end to Lake Drummond at the south, less in hope of spotting the two boys from the air than of showing them a way to follow. It finally dawned on them that the airplane's flight was a sign. "They got underneath where the plane was flying," the warden told me, "and every time it would come over, they had enough knowledge of north that they would head out. They'd kind of walk along till that plane would come back, they'd follow it again, as far as they could. Till they got up here where they said, 'Well, here's the Jericho Ditch!' "

When they got back up to Hudnell Road at Five Points about noon, a small crowd was awaiting them. "The briars had just stripped their clothes clean off, and the only thing they had on was their belt and part of their pants. And they was scratched up just like a tiger had had onto em."

Gondola on Jericho Ditch, 1856

The Nansemond warden's name was Shelton Rountree, and he reckoned that during his twenty years of working the Swamp, from roughly 1945 to 1965, about fifteen people got lost in the Great Dismal. "Some of em were lost just a short while, and a few of em—one or two of em—spent the night. What I would do was call in the hunt club that hunted that area, because they would know how many little foot trails that they had, and where the stands were and how to get to em. When you're back deep in that Swamp, if it's quiet enough you hear him holler, yell, or he shoots, it rings all over the Swamp, echoes all about, when you're deep in the Swamp. You may think he's this way and he'll be *this* way—so it's really hard to find a guy that's lost in there. When you get down in the low low part and it's thick, you can tell in somewhat direction the sound is coming, but you can't go directly to it, if it's a long ways off."

It was Shelton Rountree who, in December 1955, ran the biggest manhunt the Great Dismal ever knew. He said it was one of the worst cases of lost people he ever encountered, and he called it *Operation Swamp*.

One Friday twelve days before Christmas, the Haywoods—a sixty-six-year-old man and his eighteen-year-old son—went into the northwestern Swamp with their new squirrel dog. A little past midnight that night, a woman on White Marsh Road telephoned Rountree and told him the Haywoods had never come out of the Swamp.

By noon Saturday the warden had called on the sheriff, the Civil Air Patrol, a deer hunting club, the National Guard, and, for air assistance, the Coast Guard. The Army, Navy, Marines, and other hunt clubs joined in. The Salvation Army carried coffee and dough-nuts out to White Marsh Road. The weather was cold and gray and drizzly, and the Haywoods meanwhile were walking around in cir-cles in the Swamp trying desperately to find the field from which they had entered it. They fired seventeen shells to get the attention of helicopters they saw, to no avail, so they quit shooting and saved their ammunition.

Two of the Marines got lost, and themselves became objects of search. Once these soldiers turned up the next morning, their com-mander put them right back into the quest to find the Haywoods, telling them: "Now you go back in there and if you don't obey orders, you're gon get lost again!"

Saturday and then Sunday both ended with the Haywoods still some unknown where in the Great Dismal.

By Monday morning, Warden Rountree out on Washington Ditch found himself in command of a force of four hundred men. "We chained em off down this ditch, every man was within arm reach of the other. We said, we got to comb this woods and find those people." The searchers were to work north until noon, then either to turn back for Washington Ditch or head west for the edge of the Swamp, and it was just before they broke that they came upon the man and his son.

Cypress knees and arched black gum root, the Swamp in Pasquotank County, N.C., 1880s

The Haywoods were lying up against a tree, weak and defeated. They had fired off all their ammunition except for two cartridges: one rifle round and one shotgun shell.

"Before we lay out here and starved," the father said, "we were going to shoot ourselves."

☙

One wintry Sunday afternoon no more than a year or so after the Haywood affair, my own father took me out to ride, stopping and parking his maroon humpback '52 Dodge beside a paved road in Pasquotank just north of Elizabeth City. I have no idea what we were looking for, why we left the roadbank and walked into a tiny corner of the southernmost branch of the Swamp.

We had not been in the woods a very long time before he thought better of the exploit, and we turned to go back. The more we walked towards our car, the more water there was underfoot. Soon we were hopping from one gum hummock to another, and it was real trouble for me, for I was only eight years old. Daddy tried to carry me for a few minutes, but he couldn't keep his balance with my making him clumsy and off-center, so we stopped. After that, he only made leaps and steps that I too would be able to make, and this slowed us down even more.

He never once seemed frightened about our predicament, so I was not scared. Together we had walked in swampy woods at Big Flatty Creek in south Pasquotank, in others in Camden and Currituck, in the Nags Head Woods and in other coastal forests down on Hatteras Island at Buxton. But in those woods, a road or a body of water was never farther than a mile or so away. In this Swamp—though at most a quarter of the two thousand square miles it was in William Byrd's time—we might have walked twenty miles, northerly, before we encountered the first road. It was quite cold that Sunday, I was uncomfortable trying to perch on tree bases and root ribs and keep from getting my feet wet, and now the light was failing.

Then Daddy took another tack, and suddenly we came out of the woods, climbed up the causeway's slight incline, and looked down the road towards town at our car a quarter mile away. It was the only time in all our woods-walking that anything like this had ever happened, and in the car, once we got moving and the noisy heater-canister was whirring and pumping away, he laid his hand on my leg and patted it a couple of times and did not speak.

For a couple of gray and chilly hours many years ago, my father and I had been lost in "The Desert," turned around unawares together like so many hundreds and thousands of others in the last ten millennia, two blood-kin mortals as fallible and vulnerable as any, lost with, but not yet to, each other for a flyspeck of time in the boggy woods of the Great Dismal Swamp.

🐟

5

At Large in the Swamp

"From the depths of the Dismal Swamp, no one has ever returned."—John Hamilton Howard, *In the Shadow of the Pines*, 1906

The first time the boy who became game warden ever went into the Great Dismal, he was sixteen years old. It was 1932, and he, his brother-in-law, and some other friends went into Drummond by boat to fish for fliers, the small brown-speckled panfish with which the Lake abounds. Sweetest fish you could eat, he thought. From all the pictures he had seen, Lake Drummond was neither new nor strange to his eyes, but still he felt it a curiosity to sit in the boat and watch the way the wind played over the dark red-brown waters.

When he was seventeen he went back, this time in the dead of winter, with the same brother-in-law and two others. On a Friday afternoon they made their way up the Feeder Ditch, in a fourteen-foot homemade flat-bottomed bateau with a five-horse Johnson on it. They crossed the Lake to the northwest shore and went to a clubhouse built out over the water.

This was Sam Perry's club, and Perry, not yet married, was living there and trapping in the Swamp during the winter. That night it turned very cold, and Lake Drummond froze. The boy and his party were supposed to go home Saturday, but the ice kept them at Sam Perry's. All it did Saturday night was freeze thicker and harder. Froze up real tight, he recalled, clean on out to right just a little place in the center of the Lake.

During the night a bear came up the walkway from the shoreline to the cottage and took what meat they had hanging up outside. So now all they had to eat was cornbread and some of the muskrat Sam

Sportsman's Lodge, Lake Drummond, May 1960

Perry had trapped, and that was Sunday dinner and supper Sunday night. Monday morning they were down to cornbread and coffee. They had had plenty of wood and stayed warm, but they were tired of cards and the occasional sip of whiskey and longed to go home.

You're shut in, the boy thought. You can't walk out, can't drive out, trapper can't get out and check his traps cause they're froze under. You got to make your food last, what little you got left, not knowing how long you're gon be here. At least you're not in this corner over here camping in a tent. That would have been a mess.

Then about noon Monday it warmed up, and the wind and the waves went to work on the ice on Lake Drummond. Though it was still thick all over the Lake, the ice was broken up to where the boy's foursome thought they could make a go of it. They switched boats and motors with Sam Perry—his was flat-bottomed too, but heavier, sixteen feet with a V-bow. Perry wanted them to carry out a load of fur for him, and with five hundred 1932 dollars' worth of furs stashed under the covered bow, the four pushed off into the icy Lake, moving slowly back towards the Feeder Ditch because to run fast might have cut the sides of the boat off.

By the time they reached the spillway, the brass buckles on the boy's old fireman's raincoat were frozen, and there was ice all over the front of the coat. Brad Cherry, the spillway keeper, said to them:

"I know you boys are starved to death and want to get to a fire. Before you go out, come on in."

Cherry fed them all Brunswick stew from a pot sitting on the stove in his house there, and full of stew and coffee they then went on down the Feeder to Arbuckle Landing and Wallaceton, loaded their gear and Perry's furs into their cars, and came on home.

Stranded, young Shelton Rountree thought. We been stranded.

❦

The second time Rountree had a serious scrape in the Swamp was seven or eight years later. He had been in the service and now was working for the police department in Suffolk, and like the Haywoods he would one day rescue, he got lost squirrel hunting.

He went into the Swamp from a field off White Marsh Road between Washington Ditch and Railroad Ditch, one foggy morning before day, along an oak-grown ridge. After daylight a small flock of turkeys flew off their roost, and Rountree saw them one by one in the foggy woods. He counted three, heard a couple more go another way, and then he came down off the oak ridge into the flat of the Swamp, trying to get a count of just how many turkeys there really were in that flock and rambling around to find their roost.

In short order he was lost. He listened hard but heard no car, no truck, no train, nothing but the wind in the trees. It was damp in the flat, and Rountree tried to track himself. He had rambled so going after that flock of turkeys, though, that he couldn't track himself back to the ridge—his path just kept circling around.

The fog lifted a bit, but the day was cloudy and so gave him no directional clue. He had no compass, but he knew that west was his way back out. If I go east, he said to himself, I'm going across the Big

Feeder Ditch at Lake Drummond, outlet locks, looking east, about 1910

Swamp. Studying a gumtree high enough where the wind and rain had beaten upon it, he decided that was bound to be the north side. Then he went to what he figured was the south side, for it was smooth and less weathered, faced west, picked out a tree and started out walking. Before he reached it, he found a break in the ridge he had come in on, then hit the path he sought.

"It's a terrible feeling," Shelton Rountree told me. "I know how people feel that get lost in the woods, because I've been lost myself. I've been turned around several times, but I was really lost that morning. But I got out."

❧

Then, in the late 1940s, the police officer became game warden, working Washington's Entry, the Suffolk side, and in time the entire Virginia end of the Swamp. Warden Rountree rode the Hudnell dinkytrain two and a half miles in, got off at the end of the line at the Water Hole where the engine got its water, and walked one trail or another on through the Swamp. Sometimes he crossed up to the Norfolk and Western rail-line in the northern Swamp, other times more easterly, towards Big Entry Ditch and Deep Creek.

It was rough terrain, most of it either cut over or burned over not too long before, and thick with low bush and grass. They called these scrub openings the Lights, and the warden working his way across them many times fell through the thin crust that underground peat fires had left, fell into holes waist or shoulder deep and filled his boots with water and ice. With his gun he would pull himself back out, climb up and sit in the sun for a couple of hours in the notch of a tree or, if he were lucky, in a deer-stand, till his socks and boots were damp if not dry, and then go on again.

"I have worked a lot of days when it was miserable, snow on the ground, raining, sleeting, and so forth," he said to me. "Had a jeep I could get around in what roads there were to ride on—the Jericho Lane after they took the old tracks up, you could drive in a certain distance. But you had to walk most of the time. Now you drive all over the Swamp."

He was always on the move, eating out of cans a lot when he rode. From his friend Norman Poarch at Camp 7 he would pick up a store lunch, potted meat, some crackers—"Monkey food," he called it. "Started carrying my groceries in a regular box I had in the trunk of my car, enough groceries that I could get caught back in the Swamp during hunting season—I never would come out and drive to a restaurant someplace to eat or come home. Always just pull off the side someplace and talk to a bunch of the fellows, we'd all eat dinner. Open up a few sardines, Vienna sausage, some crackers, carry some fruit, and eat on the road. I've eat a lot on the road."

In the spring Shelton Rountree and the Norfolk County warden would once in a while go up the Feeder Ditch and check fishermen, but there was little happening on Drummond after the crappie fishing in early May. In the wintertime, when some clubs were hunting Wednesdays and Saturdays, others Thursdays and Saturdays, he was in the Great Dismal two or three days a week.

"I used to love it," he said. "Worked it, I loved it, I hunted it. I used to stay in Lake Drummond, in the camps there with different ones. I've stayed in Dewey Howell's, I've stayed in Sam Perry's, I've stayed in Rudolph Badger's, I've stayed in Jack's Camp. And I really enjoyed staying in there and hunting and fishing."

Though he did patrol the Swamp at times by himself, most of the time there were two men. "I decided it was a little bit risky going by yourself. Anything could happen."

≋

Just after sunset on the seventh of November, 1953, that anything came to pass.

From a field beside the Norfolk and Western Railroad at the northwest corner of the Swamp, Warden Rountree and his deputy, Sam Snead, had walked about three hundred yards into the Great Dismal. They heard a rustling in the leaves, someone coming at them out of the Swamp. Rountree knew there was a fence between them, and when the man approaching stopped at the fence and did not speak, Rountree figured the other had seen the two wardens silhouetted against the red late-day sky—some innate wariness of a Swamp stranger he could not see bade him take cover. Shelton Rountree sidestepped behind a large hickory tree and was just about to call out that he was the game warden when he saw the fire blaze from the stranger's shotgun.

His left arm caught an entire load of birdshot, excepting only two pellets that hit the hickory bark. Rountree, the feeling knocked out of his left side, reached under his coat, got his .38, and from the other side of the hickory shot back. The stranger had dropped a squirrel and kicked a shell out of his gun, and was retreating.

"Sam," Rountree called to the deputy off to his right, "I got to get a tourniquet on my arm. I been shot, been hit!"

Sam Snead, surprised, came right to Rountree. Blood was spinning out of the warden's wound, and while he put his thumb on a pressure point under his arm, Snead corded a handkerchief around his arm and that slowed the bleeding. As Snead tied the tourniquet tight, the stranger, who had by now backed up about twenty-five yards down the path, fired another round that cut the leaves out of the tree right over Snead's and Rountree's heads, and then he lit out.

The two men got back to their jeep, blocked a car that was headed out from the backside of the field, and saw that it was a young woman who kept house and cooked for the sheriff. Rountree bailed out, for it would be quicker to the hospital in her car, and Snead went off in the jeep to get the sheriff. The young woman was not sure how to get to the hospital, so the wounded man tried his best to give her directions. Two coal drags, on different railroads, blocked them on their way. "Suffolk's famous for trains going through," Rountree said wryly, thirty-three years later.

Sam Snead was already at the hospital's back door with a deputy sheriff, two doctors, and two nurses. They stretchered Shelton Rountree, started giving him shots—the doctor said he gave the warden enough to put two men to sleep, but he never went completely out—and began working on his arm. Rountree lay abed, critically hurt, and men and women alike who came to visit him over the coming days wept to see him so. The magazine *Virginia Wildlife* wrote movingly of Rountree's fate, for he was not only a very popular man, he was also much loved.

Shelton Rountree lost his arm, but he lived.

☙

Sam Snead had gone back to the Swamp the night of the shooting, and with a bright light he found three identical Super-X Number 6 twelve-gauge shells. The sheriff's department labeled these No. 1, No. 2, and No. 3, got an immediate lead about a hunter seen coming out of the Swamp about the time of Rountree's shooting, picked him up and sent the three shells and that hunter's double-barrel twelve-gauge to the FBI ballistics lab in Washington.

The No. 1 shell, found near the dead squirrel about fifteen paces from the hickory where Rountree was shot, was the one that got him. But the FBI after testing all three shells in the double-barrel shotgun reported that only the No. 2 shell had been fired in it. The assailant had shot twice at the game wardens, so the sheriff and others working the Rountree case now believed that shells No. 1 and 3 were from the same gun.

From here on no one could learn anything. Shelton Rountree, before he went back to work in the fields and woods and swamps of southeastern Virginia, got time to see if he could work the case any further along than the sheriff's department, the state investigator, or the FBI had been able to, but he too came up with nothing. Rountree did get an informer working for him, though, and that made all the difference.

Twenty months passed between the shooting and the morning after a session of Nansemond County Court when the informer whistled Shelton Rountree aside and gave him a tip: see about a shotgun that a woman having trouble with her husband in the Saratoga section of Suffolk hid from him, under a mattress, and later turned in to a deputy sheriff. Rountree called the off-duty deputy at home, and he had it—had it stored behind the seat of his pickup truck since the woman gave it to him.

At four A.M. the next day, the game warden and the deputy sheriff drove to Washington with the gun—a new Baystate single-barrel twelve—and the three shells. Rountree had gone to the FBI Academy, and they were anxious to help him out. By noon, the ballistics people returned this verdict on the Baystate shotgun: "If you know who owns the gun, and he hasn't never loaned it out, you got the man."

The shooter was in the Suffolk jail when Rountree got back from Washington. He was a red-haired black man, and Rountree had never seen him before. He had quite a record: his wife had filed a host of assault and battery charges and later withdrawn them; he had blinded a man in Southampton County, shooting him in the head with a shotgun; and he had even gotten so mad with a mule up in Southampton that he killed him.

Between the hearing and the trial, the shooter acted like he was crazy, landing himself in a Petersburg asylum for three weeks before being returned to stand trial. His daughter took the stand and told of her father coming in from hunting one night, hiding the shotgun behind the dresser, and telling the children to tell the law if it came to the door that no one there had been hunting that day; of being alone, just the children, in a darkened house that night as the police went through the neighborhood checking houses, all but theirs.

The shooter got eight years for assault and battery with a deadly weapon, and for maiming. He was paroled to New Jersey after three or four years and worked up there. Once he came home to Suffolk and tried to buy a resident hunting license from a deputy clerk, Shelton Rountree's wife, but she recognized him from court, knew he was a nonresident, and refused him.

He moved back to Suffolk after his parole was up and died of a skin disease not long after his return. Shelton Rountree never did talk with him, but Sam Snead, the other man who might have lost his life the day the game warden lost his arm, came across him rabbit hunting one day and checked his license.

"Wasn't that a little strange for Sam Snead?" I asked Shelton Rountree.

"No, I don't think so. That fellow'd pulled his time, paid his debt. Sam just checked him, wished him luck, and went on."

*

One of the game warden's many friends was an old-time trapper named Evick, who worked the Swamp's north side until he died twenty years ago. He lived with his wife in a small house behind the big homeplace at Spring Farm, the last farm down a south-running lane off U.S. 58 just past Magnolia on the way to Norfolk.

Evick took two days to run his fifty-trap line, going into the Swamp from behind his house, crossing the Norfolk and Western Railroad tracks, then the powerline that paralleled it, on down into the timber. He carried with him enough food for his lunch and his supper, and for his breakfast the next morning after he had spent the night in a hollow tree that was his trapping camp.

"The stump part was huge," Shelton Rountree recalled. "He made him a little room in that hollow, went in there and pulled out all the rotten wood, and fixed him up a little room. He would crawl in that tree at night. And I don't think any of the hunters ever knew where it was, because he was the only man that ever trapped, went that far back in there. They might have seen the tree, but they never noticed it.

"Evick caught a lot of fur. He was interested mainly in raccoon and mink, and he was good at mink, brown mink, black mink. The black mink was much higher than the brown, at the time. See, the fur business runs with the style of what the women wear. If the style comes along that you got fur collars on your coats, then your mink's a little higher, your fur goes up. Back in the old days, when the college boys wore coonskin coats down to their ankles almost, back in the Depression, coonhides were selling for ten dollars, and you couldn't find a coon track nowhere in two square miles out in the country in Carolina. They caught em all!

"Evick would bet on his coon and mink. Very seldom would he fool with fox—fox hide back then was a dollar, two dollars. Now fox hides're thirty-five dollars, but there're not too many in the Swamp. We used to catch mink from down in the Swamp to right on out to the edge of the highway. The ditches that ran through those fields, those mink would follow those ditch lines for food. And he caught about as many mink along the openings as he did down deep in the Swamp. And muskrat—he's caught a lot of muskrat."

One November Shelton Rountree got Evick to help him go after an illegal, out-of-season trapper who had set sixteen traps out over several miles. In hipwaders from dawn to dusk the pair traipsed the Swamp, prodding with poles the underwater sets till they had gotten them all. Once the warden had served the summons, though, the outlaw trapper fled Virginia on the first Trailways he could catch.

"Back before they opened all these ditches up, the water level in the Swamp in some places was from ankle deep to up above your knees year round—unless it was a mighty dry year," Rountree said. "During the summer, it would dry out, but as soon as you started having rains in the fall then your water was back standing again. There's otter getting in the Swamp now, with those canals, but there were few otter back then. They never cared anything about a weasel, their hides wasn't any good.

"And no beaver at all, back then, but we got a few beaver coming in this area, started maybe back five, ten years ago. In the Suffolk area here now you got beaver, and there'll eventually be beaver in the Swamp. But I never saw beaver in the Swamp, as long as I worked it.

"Southampton County's getting quite a few beaver along the railroad tracks in the swamps. Union Bag-Camp has a place up there they're having problems with the beaver, damming up the water and killing the young pine trees. They had to get some trappers out of New York to come down and catch em—local trappers didn't get the bid."

🜚

"Most of your older hunters are gone," Rountree remarked to me, and not without regret, since these were men like him for whom the Swamp was a great and wondrous being, a wilderness that took them in and gave them its treasures of wildlife and spirit in a measure commensurate with their understanding of it, their devotion to it. In the main they were men born at its edge who drank in its essential and seductive mystery with their mothers' milk.

There was Earl Bass of Yadkin and the Yadkin Hunt Club, son of the Nansemond Indian Chief Jesse Bass, who kept as many as five dozen deerhounds and took doctors and lawyers into the big timber after deer and bear.

There was Dewey Howell, who drove just as many hounds as Bass for the old Lady of the Lake and Jack's Hunt Clubs, who more than once watched an osprey snatch a fish out of Drummond only to drop that dinner for a larger and greedier eagle, Dewey Howell who learned as he cut his father's shirttail for a missed shot at a deer that the wily father was wearing the son's shirt, who saved the last man of three from freezing and drowning as the other two had in a rough winter's Lake thirty years ago, who now deals in antiques from the Auction Barn at Magnolia on the Swamp's north side.

There was Joe Barnes of the Black Cats Hunt Club, a man who learned his trapping and hunting when he was a boy in the 1920s from an ancient Indian-looking black man named Dick Hawk. Barnes was a man whose tent-ridge collapsed beneath the heavy, March 1927 snow but who nonetheless tented and trapped all winter on Portsmouth Ditch two years later and at the tender age of sixteen netted nearly two thousand dollars, a man who thought nothing of carrying his high-grade furs all the way to Chicago, there to make the Fuchs and Rodgers and Taylor fur companies pay him top dollar.

And there was Wallace Griffin, who hunted the Washington Ditch area from the late 1800s till his death in the 1940s, and Wallace Williams, who live-trapped bobcats on Portsmouth Ditch as recently as the late 1960s, and Toni Darden, who was about the only woman that Shelton Rountree remembered as a Swamp hunter.

"She owned a big mansion up here on Broad Street," he said, "right here in Suffolk, just down Nansemond River a little ways there, what they call Oak Island. Nice home up there—she had saddle horses. She belonged to the Ed Gillette club, yeah, Magnolia Hunt Club. She'd drive over to Magnolia and go down to the edge of the Swamp. And she fox hunted a lot. Never got married. Daddy left her plenty money."

Someone should sing a slow, blue-yodeling song for all these hunters and trappers, coursers of the great wilderness morass, one breaking occasionally into loud chopmouth choruses for all the dogs of the Dismal, all those hundreds and thousands of hounds turned loose at the Swamp's edge or put out from and gathered back into boats at the Lake's sunken shores, for all their treeing, cornering, giving chase, getting lost, and staying lost while owners waiting up in the night blew thin wailing blasts on horns like two centuries ago, or ten, for all the dogs that went out and came back, and for all those that did not. Someone should sing that song, long and now loud and now low, and someday, I believe, I will.

⇜

All the Swampers weren't hunters, either. I asked Shelton Rountree about John Lynn, gatekeeper to the Swamp for Union Camp, who lived in a house Camp built for him at Five Points at the Swamp's northwest corner, and for whom Lynn Ditch is named.

"Oh, yeah," Rountree said, "Ol' man John was a catbird, he was a

Warden Rountree checking fishing licenses, Washington Ditch, May 1960

real old Swamper, he loved the Swamp. He kept the ditches, kept em cleaned out at the gates on the ditches. Wife lived there with him. They were real nice people. He loved the woods. Only time he'd come out, he'd come out and get groceries, and go back. And I forgot what nationality he was, but he couldn't talk real plain. He worked up north, in the north country, years and years, came down, went to work for Union Bag. And he'd always been in the woods all of his life. He's quite a character. Oh, yeah, he'd tell you some jokes. He never hunted.

"While he was living there, he had a couple of cub bear that fed, would come into his backyard and pick up food that he'd leave out back of the house there, at the garbage can for em. Called em his pets. And that fall when the deer season opened, right up the Jericho Ditch here a little ways, up in a big acorn tree, one of the hunters killed one of those cubs. And I had to go down and give him a ticket for killing a bear underweight—at that time the weight limit was seventy-five pounds. And I'll never forget, Mister Lynn says,

" 'I'm glad you got him—he killed my pet. And I don't know where the other one is, somebody'll probably kill him too.'

"But they didn't, cause the club told the boys not to shoot those cub bear, and they didn't shoot the other one. The boy got excited I guess, shot the bear. He said he thought it was bigger than it was, looked bigger anyway up a tree, and the tree wadn't a hundred yards behind the house, where he killed the bear."

🐟

Liquormakers were at large in here, too. An Elizabeth City man once told me of liquor being hauled by automobile caravan up through the Swamp to Norfolk, that it was coming from a still down in Tyrrell County, south of Albemarle Sound, a still so big and operating in swamps there with such impunity its operators called its workers in for their shifts by steamwhistle. He said the bootleggers would blockade the long straight and narrow Highway 17, the Canalbank Highway, at both ends and then roar their ten or twenty cars and trucks northward to market unbothered and unimpeded.

A couple of weeks after the Swamp-loving writer Charles Stansbury flew a Curtiss Seagull into the Dismal and landed on Lake Drummond on New Year's Day, 1921, a newspaper editor in Norfolk said to him:

"I doubt if you know the greatest peril that confronted you when your seaplane rested on Lake Drummond in the heart of the Swamp."

"What was it?" Stansbury asked.

"The danger of being shot. The Great Dismal swarms with moonshiners. They are not society people; they certainly do not relish sudden visits from strange gentlemen from the sky. Perhaps you were out of range; but, for the sake of your friends, please don't go there that way again."

Virginia forester George Dean, while fighting fire in the Swamp's north end during the summer of 1930, was walking along a two-foot wooden conduit—one of Portsmouth's city waterlines—that ran just south of the railroads and parallel to them. When he spied a wooden plug in the pipe, one "fashioned from well-weathered wood that matched closely the color of the water main," he then followed a worn path two hundred feet south into the Swamp, where he found a big clearing.

"In the opening," Dean later recalled, "were several mash boxes with mash well-ripened, a twenty-gallon still, cans, and other necessary equipment. Every still must have water, which was a scarce commodity out in that dry reed-patch. The operators had ingeniously solved their problem by running an ordinary garden hose out to the water main, bored a hole and tapped in the hose. When not in use the hose was withdrawn from the water main and the path."

Ornithologist Brooke Meanley, who has been roaming the Great Dismal since the late 1950s, happened upon rusting ruins of stills in the course of his work along Cypress Creek near Cypress Chapel and in the evergreen shrub bog at the east end of Corapeake Ditch. And Shelton Rountree said he regularly came across working setups while making his rounds.

"If I passed a whiskey still, I saw it and didn't see it, see what I mean? That wadn't in our line of work. Unless it was a still large enough that I thought the man was making a lot of profit, maybe he shouldn't be doing, I would turn it over to the A.B.C. board. Cause people knew if a still was turned in that I was in the woods, see, lot of times. And a lot of em I didn't mind turning in, but some of em I wouldn't—little coffee-pot still, man was making a little for himself, maybe for his neighbor, he was carrying in maybe a gallon a week. Little small rigs, there were several of those along the Swamp."

These stills, Rountree said, would typically be in the Swamp woods behind fields that bordered the Dismal along its northern and western edges. "And they were local people, they wadn't running no big rigs. Some of em was older people. I don't want to say they were all black, there was some whites, some of em I didn't know who the owners was. I wouldn't stay around em long enough to find out who the owner of the still was." He never actually saw anyone working any of these stills, but Shelton Rountree said:

"I have seen one or two within a hundred yards of a still, and I knew that still belonged to him. I met one fellow that had five gallons of gas back in the woods, and I jokingly asked him,

" 'You don't have a car back here, you're not out of gas, you can't drive a car in here.' And he said,

" 'No, a friend of mine wanted me to bring him some gas, and I took this footpath and got lost and I'm headed back out round here to his house.' And I said,

" 'Well, that's a good story, you go ahead.' If you do run into a person, and you got to talk to him, talk to him in a way that you leave him friendly, and he's gone, see. Because I'm in that woods all the time myself, in and out, and if I know where a still is, I'm not going next to it. If it's a big rig, yeah, I'll turn him in. But there's no big rigs, never a big rig in the Swamp. They were all little stuff, small stuff."

That seems mostly to have been the case, but two months after I visited Shelton Rountree in Suffolk, there was a raid on a still way on the other side of the Swamp, down in North Carolina near South Mills. The man the Carolina liquor agents collared was the well-known tee-totaling bootlegger Alvin Sawyer, a man my father got off on a liquormaking charge in the 1950s, telling him after the trial: "I got you off this time, Alvin, but if they catch you again, I can't help you."

But they caught him again, and he did four years in federal prison. And in January 1987 the law got Alvin Sawyer once more. The sixty-nine-year-old Sawyer had been running a two-thousand-gallon still on a slough off Pasquotank River. It was the largest moonshine still ever seized in the Great Dismal Swamp, and the biggest white-liquor bust, period, in North Carolina in ten years.

❧

It was a misting and drizzly gray December morning I spent with Shelton Rountree at his home in Suffolk, much like the days, he said, when he and the great army of searchers were out in the Swamp looking for the Haywoods, father and son. We sat in the kitchen and drank coffee, and I noticed propped up on the counter near the percolator a platter with a weeping fish on it, and this legend beneath:

"The only sad sole allowed in this kitchen is on a platter."

The former game warden, then seventy, was quite a sanguine man, forthright and merry at the same time. Across the kitchen table he spread old articles, a journal, a photograph of the Reynoldson School down in Gates County, North Carolina. "I lived at Reynoldson, in Carolina, till I was fifteen years old," he said. "My mother boarded schoolteachers. I think we had twelve teachers. That was some school during its day."

Reynoldson, a preparatory school for Wake Forest College, got going before the Civil War. It was housed in a large three-story building with an octagonal cupola and high-columned porches wrapping all the way around. In the photograph there were several dozen students posed before it, and down front, sitting Indian-style and smiling at the camera, was Shelton Rountree, age seven.

Another artifact he laid upon the table was an X ray of his left arm, full of shot right at and above the elbow. It was a chilling picture to stare at and consider, but the one-armed man had something else to show me: a long white envelope he shook and rattled and handed to me. "I got one No. 6 shot in there, you can feel it right there. That was in this arm, the hospital failed to get it," he laughed. His handwriting on the envelope read:

"Stayed in arm for 25 years. From November 7th, 1953, it worked itself out June 18th, 1977."

"I just keep it for a souvenir," Shelton Rountree said, and I reflected, No sad soul in this kitchen. But he had told me earlier that it had been some years since he was in the Great Dismal, and I asked him if he missed going in there.

"I did for a long time, yeah. I like Lake Drummond, I'd like to stay. But now it's under government control . . . you got so many rules and regulations that I give it up. You don't know when you're doing right and when you're doing wrong. If you plan to go tomorrow and it rains, well, you're not supposed to use the roads when it rains. All the regulations like that, see, that bothers you.

"And I finally figured at my age, why should I ramble round in there? So I don't go in there anymore. I don't say I'll *never* go. I may take a ride down there in the spring, I may go down to Lake Drummond in the spring of the year. I may get a permit to drive on in. Might go fishing in the Lake."

6

Canalbank Life

> "As the Dismal must be drained by the help of canals, to
> be cut from the northern to the southern rivers, there
> will be a safe and easy communication, by water, betwixt
> Virginia and North Carolina, to the manifest advantage
> of both."—William Byrd II, "Proposal to Drain the
> Dismal Swamp," circa 1730

The most that most folks ever see of the Great
Dismal is along the straight stretch of U.S. 17,
the George Washington Highway, between Deep
Creek, Virginia, and South Mills, North Carolina. Or rather, the *two*
straightaways: the slender road runs south-southwest for eleven
miles, makes a seemingly inexplicable obtuse bend at a place long
called The Angle, then runs south-southeast another eleven miles.

Paralleling this roadway, a few feet off to the west, is the Dismal
Swamp Canal, the broad, shallow, juniper-water ditch that is the
oldest extant man-excavated waterway in America. On the far side,
the west side, of the Canal is a dense curtain of green, reeds and
maples and big pines, and that curtain is the eastern edge of the
Great Dismal, implacably obscuring any view of the vast wilderness
beyond.

When the dark water fills the Canal trough, and it does not always
anymore, then the Canal and the road it caused to be look no
different to me now than they did when I was a little boy thirty-five
years ago. There is nothing about these thoroughfares at the edge of
the Swamp to suggest that the Canal at various times concerned
Washington, Jefferson, Monroe, Jackson, the Union and Confederate Armies, tens of thousands of boatmen, timbermen, truckfarm-
ers, or that it was a controversial project in its inception and con-

struction that dragged out over decades, or that it was a dangerous and somewhat debauched avenue.

But it did, and it was.

⤸

Twenty years and the American Revolution separated George Washington from his time in the Swamp when Canal talk started up in the 1780s. Nothing had yet come of his Land Company adventure in the northwest quadrant of the Swamp, and when Hugh Williamson of North Carolina broached the notion of a ship canal to Washington in 1784, the future president was ambivalent.

On the one hand Washington felt the project "would in my opinion be tedious and attended with an expense which might prove discouraging." All the same, he wrote Williamson in late March of that year, "I have long been satisfied of the practicability of opening communication between the waters which empty into Albemarle Sound thro' Drummond's Pond and the Waters of Elizabeth or Nansemond Rivers."

Two weeks before Christmas 1784, Williamson wrote Thomas Jefferson in Paris, still pushing the Dismal Swamp Canal but worrying in print over political backlash in the Old North State: "People near Edenton are afraid that a canal from Pasquotank River, through Drummond's Lake, would deprive that town of its small remains of Trade, and the people of Pasquotank River who would be profitted by the canal have not Enterprise enough to go on with Work."

Jefferson was undaunted, replying two months later: "I am glad to find you think of me in the affair of the Dismal. It is the only speculation in my life I have decidedly wished to be engaged in."

Though the 1784 Nicholas Forster survey of "The course of the intended Canal thro' the Dismal Swamp" put the route several miles east of Drummond's Pond, bending westerly towards the Lake to avoid Balyhack Branch, headwaters of the Northwest River, George Washington warmed to the Canal idea. By late 1785 he was writing James Madison and expressing his pleasure that "our Assembly were in a way of adopting a mode for establishing the cut between Elizabeth River and Pasquotank."

With second-term Governor Patrick Henry pushing it in Virginia, and with North Carolina's Governor Caswell at least overcoming his reservations enough to present Virginia's proposal to the Carolina Assembly, the Dismal Swamp Canal plan moved forward in both legislatures. Virginia voted it in on the first of December, 1787, and North Carolina risked what one opponent predicted would be a "dwindling into fishing towns" because of the Canal and finally let the Canal Act get by on third reading in 1790. Both bodies had approved the Canal on a subscription basis, so now began the slow process of raising money to hire the shovels. George Washington bought two hundred shares, the state of Virginia seventy, and North Carolina none.

It was 1793 before digging began.

Three years later, when the Duke de la Rochefoucauld-Liancourt toured through the Great Dismal country, he was impressed with the five miles already dug in each of the two states. But he was even more impressed by the engineering procedures of the enterprise. "What must appear surprizing, is that, for this canal which already seems in such a state of forwardness, no levels have been taken. It is not yet known what number of locks may be necessary, and even whether any will be requisite. Consequently it is impossible to ascertain what may be the expense of completing it, or even whether the success of the undertaking can be depended on. It is thus almost all the public works are carried on in America, where there is a total want of men with talents in the arts."

Its construction was "a slow nibbling process," in the words of Canal historian Alexander Crosby Brown, a process characterized by delays, by extensions of projected completion dates by the two legislatures, by lack of money, and by lack of labor. Though the worker had to show up with his own axe, spade, or shovel, an 1808 solicitation in the *Norfolk Gazette and Public Ledger* pledged to laborers "good wholesome food and the usual quantity of whisky per diem." The digging had gone on from both ends towards the middle, and when these two ditchings met each other and joined the Albemarle Sound with the Chesapeake Bay in 1805, four miles of the Canal were at half the prescribed width.

There was some grade of trouble all the time. The great 1806 fire in the Swamp clogged the Canal, both above and below water, with trees. And there was competition over water levels: those who were trying to float shingles out of the Swamp over the Canal needed more water than those who were still digging on it. An 1808 high water drove Samuel Proctor, the digging director in North Carolina, to "cut loose that lock at Mr. Spences in order to get the water off." Proctor reported to the Canal Company president: "But that man known by the name of Isaac Place—goes at the dead hour of the night & stops it—if some measure is not taken to prevent his meddling with that end of the canal it will never be done." Isaac Pleas, in his own report to the president, dismissed Proctor's hydraulic practices and claimed he was under personal attack: "Yet I did not think the spleen would be carri'd so far as to Injure me, until of lately there has appeared some striking features in the conduct of Samuel Proctor that show he would wantonly do me what Injury lays in his power."

The Canal, though completed, was "little more than a muddy ditch," according to historian Brown. Only shingle flats floated over it in its earliest years, and one outraged shareholder declared to the company by open letter in an April 1808 *Norfolk Gazette and Public Ledger*: "You have marked the course of the canal it is true—you have made an indifferent road, and a boat can swim empty four or five miles in the center of the Dismal Swamp! All this you have performed in little more than sixteen years!"

The company had realized by 1804 that the Canal was going to require waters from Lake Drummond—an eventuality foreseen and legislated for by the Virginia Assembly in 1787—to float boats of any size and substance. On August 4, 1812, eighteen citizens of Norfolk County met with the sheriff and gazed Swampward at the 300-foot by three-and-a-half-mile strip of Dismal they were about to condemn, in order that a small canal—the Feeder Ditch—could drain

Drummond into the main Canal. The sheriff's jury appraised the necessary lands at a penny an acre, and the Canal company paid its dollar and a quarter for the strip and cut the Feeder that year.

In June of 1814, James Smith's twenty-ton craft came down the Roanoke River from Scotland Neck, sailed out onto Albemarle Sound at Batchelor Bay, made it up the Pasquotank, rounding the Narrows at Elizabeth City and winding through the Moccasin Track, thence north to Deep Creek and the south branch of the Elizabeth River, a big Carolina boat now in Norfolk bearing bacon and brandy.

The first ship had made passage through the Dismal Swamp Canal.

🦐

The Virginia legislature approved raffles as a fund-raising tool for the Canal in 1816, and there were three of them—in 1819, 1820, and 1829—in short order. The federal government took an increased interest in the Canal. President James Monroe, along with Secretary of War John C. Calhoun and others, toured the Canal and Lake Drummond in 1818. By 1829, the United States government had bought half of the outstanding shares in the enterprise, and in that year President Andrew Jackson came down on a barge from Norfolk's Gosport Navy Yard to see the big long ditch. On the Canalbank, the President and his compatriots picnicked agreeably, dining on Virginia ham, smoked beef and tongues, cypress shingles serving as plates. Old Hickory pronounced upon the moment:

"Reminds me of the days when I used to eat all my meals sitting on a log in the woods."

Now there were stagecoaches running regularly up and down the Canalbank, making steamboat connections in Norfolk and Elizabeth City. And the Canal was full of shingle lighters and timber rafts, schooners and sloops, and the schooner-rigged barges of freighters called the Virginia and North Carolina Transportation Company. There were improvements around and below the Canal's locks at either end, the Gilmerton Division at Deep Creek in 1843, Turner's

Cut bypassing the "Moccasin Track" of Joyce's Creek from South Mills to the Pasquotank River in 1856. In this middle third of the nineteenth century, the Dismal Swamp Canal had its heyday.

Then, too, it had its competition. Train lines that prefigured both the Seaboard Air Line and the Norfolk and Western cut across the northern Swamp. The Portsmouth and Roanoke Railroad, a 56½"-gauge line laid on a wooden trestle above the Swamp, was completed through to Suffolk in the summer of 1834. Just before Christmas, 1841, Sir Charles Lyell rode these rails, marveling that the "enormous quagmire" was "higher than the surrounding firm ground," and that "the railway itself, when traversing the Great Dismal, is six to seven feet higher than where it passes over dry ground, near to Suffolk and Portsmouth." In the 1850s, William Mahone, a twenty-seven-year-old V.M.I. engineer, slammed the Norfolk and Petersburg Railroad through the Swamp. Mahone, a future railroad president, Confederate brigadier general, and United States senator, cut a hundred-foot-wide slash, piled cypress and cedar in the center of the strip, and earthed them over for roadbed that still serves the N&W.

Of the coming of the railroads to such remote reaches, Henry David Thoreau wrote in *Walden* in 1854: "Far through unfrequented woods on the confines of towns, where once only the hunter penetrated by day, in the darkest night dart these bright saloons without the knowledge of their inhabitants; this moment stopping at some brilliant station-house in town or city, where a social crowd is gathered, the next in the Dismal Swamp, scaring the owl and fox."

By 1859 there was another whole thoroughfare starting to steal trade from the Dismal Swamp Canal: the Albemarle and Chesapeake Canal, connecting the Elizabeth River in Virginia with Currituck Sound in North Carolina, a shorter, easier route whose single lock, at Great Bridge, Virginia, was the largest on the continent when it was finished. Confederates fleeing northward after the fall of Elizabeth City in February 1862 burned the C.S.S. *Appomattox*—two inches too wide to go through the South Mills locks—and cut the Dismal Swamp Canal's banks to drain it down; they attempted to hold the A&C Canal as well, but after their defeat at the Battle of

Sybilla, *a Philadelphia yacht covered with waterfowl from a southern hunt, one of the first ships through the renewed Canal, about 1900*

Camden in April 1862 and the Union occupation of Norfolk in May, the Confederate effort around the Swamp and main Canal was one of guerrilla skirmish, bridge burning, and ambush. At the end of the Civil War, the little-tended, unmaintained Dismal Swamp Canal was a ruin and was unable in the 1870s to service its debt at a time when the A&C Canal was running nearly a hundred thousand dollars in the black.

A new outfit—the Lake Drummond Canal and Water Company—bought the Canal in 1892, when the Canal could no longer float a boat of three-foot draft. A Philadelphia contractor named McManus got the reconstruction job and out of wood built in the Canal's Summit Level, not far from Lake Drummond, three dipper dredges and four large hydraulic dredges—the former to go along removing surface material and breaking up roots and rough bottom to a depth of five feet, the latter to follow the dippers and, with their vertical cutting shafts of fifty knife-arms each, fired by hundred-

Dismal Swamp Canal at South Mills, N.C., about 1900

horse engines, cut the renewed Canal to a uniform depth of ten feet, forty feet across at the bottom, sixty feet at the top. From the depths below the Summit Level, the hydraulic dredges brought up Miocene Age fossils, coral, and foot-long oystershells weighing five pounds apiece.

The work began February 15, 1896, and when the new Canal opened October 14, 1899, there was a floating banquet aboard the southbound steamboat *Ocean View*, another when this steamboat and a fleet of fellow celebratory vessels reached Elizabeth City that night. The Canal's four levels had become one, with locks now only at Deep Creek and South Mills, and a new heyday was on. The Dismal Swamp Canal, down in 1880 to 6,700 tons of freight compared to the A&C Canal's 400,000, by 1906 beat out the A&C 340,000 tons to 95,000. But the federal government's purchase of the A&C a few years later, and its no-toll policy on it, burst the Dismal Swamp Canal's brief new bubble. In 1929, the government bought the Swamp Canal—whose investment in 1857 had stood at $1,150,000 and whose late 1890s rebuilding had run another million—for half a million dollars, redredged and repaired it, and found it extremely useful strategically during the Atlantic Coast submarine threat of World War II. Postwar plans for the channel through the

Swamp, as diverse as one to make the Canal an industrial corridor, an American Ruhr, and another to make of it an oddball botanical splendor, a twenty-two-mile floral display, have come to naught. In the late 1950s, the Corps of Engineers began an effort to close the Canal down altogether, as commercial traffic had become nearly nonexistent and almost all the water-intensive lockages—a million and a quarter gallons each time—were for pleasure craft. That effort continues today, in the face of strong political pressure from northeastern North Carolina—my old hometown of Elizabeth City, particularly—to keep it open.

Fred Fearing, a spry retired mailman in Elizabeth City and old friend of my family, has in recent years with another man been meeting incoming sailboats and yachts down at the Elizabeth City docks and greeting them with flowers and champagne. When I asked him one night in August of 1985 about the Canal's being unnavigable and nearly dry, he exploded bitterly at the Corps, which had reported drought and leaky wickets at the locks as the cause of the Canal's low-water closing.

"The sonofabitches!" Fearing said. "The bastards! They're draining it down cause they want to shut it up for good. Oldest continuously used man-made waterway in American history, and this is how it ends up. Bastards!"

⮜

The Canalbank's "indifferent road," once it reaches Elizabeth City, has long been known as Road Street. On the northeast corner of Road and Main stands a hotel of oxblood brick, the New Southern Hotel put up just after World War I for drummers and coastal excursionists, and on the Road Street side of the hotel was a small barber shop.

Harry Umphlett, an owlish and unhurried man with hornrimmed glasses, cut my hair here when I was a boy. Often he would be alone in the shop, standing quietly and unemployed before shelves of talcums and lotions and candy-colored toilet waters, when I showed up after school for a trim. But sometimes I would have to wait, and

Dismal Swamp Canal at Arbuckle Landing, Va., after the washout of the South Mills locks, Saturday afternoon, October 17, 1920

to endure not unpleasantly the grown-up talk of some shopkeeper with an unlit cigar in his hand, or held between his teeth as he spoke. The back wall always had an insurance-company calendar on it, its artwork a big two-by-three-foot color lithograph of ducks and geese coming in to land in some marshy place, so the rear of Mister Umphlett's shop really looked like it was a window on the riverine world all around us, the Pasquotank, Camden, and Currituck.

I liked it there, all the more because Mister Umphlett had taken a shine to me back when I was four and five, still sitting on the padded crossboard he plunked across the barberchair for young children, and practicing my states of the Union with my mother while awaiting my turn under the shears. But all the years I went to Mister Umphlett's shop, weekly to stay neat, I never knew that he was anything other than a barber, a trimmer and groomer of heads of hair.

In fact, Harry Umphlett was a marrying man, a justice of the peace, a quick joiner of lives who with the aid of a sidestreet while-you-wait bloodtest lab doubtless did far more of a wedding business than all the local churches combined. Such was the high level of excitement attending this hasty game that I know of at least one occasion on which a couple of friends of the bride and groom got carried away by the spirit of the wedding they were witnessing and were themselves married by Mister Umphlett an hour later. Umphlett in this capacity was now heir to a hundred-and-fifty-year-old practice in those parts, whereby folks dropped down from Virginia to tie a prompt and unimpeded Carolina knot.

The original Gretna Green was Major William Farange's hostelry, the Brickhouse Plantation on the Canal two and a half miles south of the Carolina and Virginia boundary line, and the original money-making man in the marriage trade was Squire Willie McPherson, the wealthiest citizen of Camden County when he died in 1835. Not all the marriages in Camden took place at Major Farange's, nor was Squire Willie the only joiner, but this was a popular Camden combination in the early 1800s.

A man named Mordecai, surveying in the Great Dismal in the spring of 1828, wrote his sister complaining about sinking knee-deep in "the pathless bog," but also carrying on to her about the blessed event he had happened to witness at Major Farange's. A horse and carriage roared up, and out of the carriage jumped a sailor, obviously awaiting someone. Next came a man on a galloping horse, and, after some quick talk between these two, the sailor brought forth from the carriage a "blushing damsel and her female relative." Squire McPherson—whose name everyone pronounced "Make fashion"—then "arranged the confused parties to his satisfaction," wrote Mordecai, and presented the sailor a bride with whose name "the bridegroom seemed to have been till that moment unacquainted."

Marriage with a twist was less than unusual in Canal country. One newspaper remarked of a Carolina wedding: "The fortunate groom was just nineteen and the fair bride was just forty-five." And the marital experience of Mason Culpepper, state senator from Camden in 1822, was worthy of note. Culpepper's family had built and operated the first locks—Culpepper Locks—on the Dismal Swamp Canal, but such enmity existed between Mason and his father Peter that the father left a substantial estate to his wife and eight other children, excepting Mason alone. Mason fought the will and won, which fight involved Squire Willie McPherson refusing to qualify as executor and the court subsequently naming the black sheep Mason

Lake Drummond Hotel, with the Lady of the Lake, *a sternwheel steamboat, north-bound on the Dismal Swamp Canal, 1831*

as estate administrator. All the internecine strife took its toll on Mason, though, for his obituary in early 1826 read in part:

"This melancholy event was preceded by the death of one wife and his marriage to another—all happening within the compass of six weeks! He lived a disconsolate widower three weeks, and a happy groom three more."

Major Farange had operated without competition for nearly three decades, since his purchase of Brickhouse Plantation in October 1802. His monopoly ended in January 1830, when Isaiah Rogerson first advertised in Norfolk the long, boundary-line–straddling Lake Drummond Hotel, calling it "large and commodious, being 128 feet long and having eight separate chambers, with fireplaces."

Isaiah Rogerson was dead by August. "We have no particulars as to the death," said Norfolk's *American Beacon*. In early September, Daniel Rogerson advertised that he now had the Hotel rented and open. Major Farange fought back—two days after Daniel Rogerson's announcement, the Major published a complaint over rumors that were being floated about his having quit keeping "a house of entertainment." He still had a going concern, said the Major, "at the same old place where he has kept one for twenty-eight years past."

Major Farange was by far the more durable and reliable Swamp hotelier. By the time another three months had passed, Daniel Rogerson had vanished, and the Lake Drummond Hotel was up for sale before the end of its first year, with this proclamation:

"This establishment (being situated on the N.C.–Va. line, one half the building in each state), is in a superior degree, calculated to render facilities for matrimonial and duelistical engagements and should the purchaser become a magistrate, the facilities would be much increased though rather detrimental in the latter. Indeed it is a stand fully applicable for all the purposes of life, as eating, drinking, sleeping, marrying, duelling, &., &., in all its varieties."

Another Rogerson, William this time, bought the place in 1831, but living in a hotel beside the Swamp road and being a friend to man suited him no better than his predecessors. By September 1831 Abner Williams, proprietor of the Indian Queen Hotel in Elizabeth City, had acquired at least the North Carolina side of the Lake Drummond Hotel and set his son Amalek up running it. Amalek Williams dealt quickly with the twin concerns of the hotel's reputation and rates, advertising:

"By the establishment of this Hotel, the vulgar epithet of Gretna's lost; for Hymen here has raised his holy fane, where the bright torch before the altar burns, and the reverent priest unites the happy pair." He bragged on the efficiency of it all, too. "Marriage parties can at all times be accommodated to their utmost wish—in half an hour after their arrival 'the blushing bride salutes her wedded lord.' "

As to the Lake Drummond Hotel's "Schedule of Rates," Amalek Williams set the following:

Dinner	50 cents
Supper or breakfast	37½ cents
Lodging	12½ cents
Board	
Daily	$ 1.00
Weekly	$ 4.50
Monthly	$18.00

Horse	
Single Feed	25 cents
Daily	75 cents
Weekly	$ 3.00
Monthly	$12.00

Whatever Amalek's designs were towards setting a higher tone for his family's Swamp spa, the Hotel in the Great Dismal came to be called the Halfway House, and its real reputation was one more of rowdiness than reverent priests. After running the place for three years, Amalek turned over the reins to his brother-in-law, Wilson Lamb, who carried on until the owner, Abner Williams, died in 1839 and the Lake Drummond Hotel was sold as a part of his estate settlement.

How much real violence attended the state line elopement trade, or existed side by side with it, is hard to say. But because of its boundary-straddling situation, wrote Canal historian Brown, "Fugitives from justice in Virginia reposed as contentedly in the North Carolina end of the building as did North Carolina fugitives on the Virginia side." News of only one Halfway House duel—a face-off between two Greenville, North Carolina, lawyers—ever made it into print, the *American Beacon*'s October 1847 report that a Mister Yelloby had killed a Mister Harris there. A little fact went a long way towards feeding fear and apprehension, though, and here this hotel was, as close to the middle of the dread Dismal as most pilgrims cared to go.

It was a good climate for fear, and long had been. During May and June of 1802, a black outlaw named Tom Copper, who was believed to have a Swamp stronghold, stirred fears of Negro insurrection. Samuel Perkins, the Yankee tutor who journeyed through the Dismal in late October 1817, reported the general fright over Swamp travel, a fearful respect accorded runaway slaves who ventured forth from their wilderness hideouts as plunderers and highwaymen. In June of 1823 a number of blacks fired three times on Henry Culpepper when he answered their knock on the front door of his home, near Major Farange's on the Canal. Culpepper was unharmed that time, but one Friday daybreak two months later, a black man who had stayed the night at Culpepper's asked him for "some liquor." On the way to his dramshop outside, Culpepper stopped seven slugs from the two guns of assailants unknown and died four days later.

Nor were race or robbery always in the mix—just before Christmas, 1845, near the South Mills lock, James Sawyer murdered his paramour, a Camden County girl named Catherine, "plunged his dagger into her breast," said the *American Beacon*, then lit out, no doubt for the tall timber of the nearby Swamp, if not the northern end of the Halfway House. In our time, the middle of November 1987, a Chesapeake, Virginia, man named Bonney shot his daughter twenty-seven times and dumped her nude body beside the Canal, just below the Carolina border. Since he was "Satan" and his dead grandmother as well, Bonney pled multiple-personality insanity, but an Elizabeth City jury said murder in the first degree. The fate of the 1845 stabber is less well known, for the Swamp has long since swallowed him whole.

"It was on a cold morning of February that we entered the crazy machine which performs the duty of a 'stage' between Norfolk, Virginia, and Elizabeth City, North Carolina," wrote a Scotsman on Southern tour in 1850. "Our journey for more than half the distance lay along the range of the Dismal Swamp. . . . The road was monotonous; no change of scenery enlivened it; the canal and tall dark cypresses flanked our right, and wild waste-looking corn-fields or tangled bushes our left. . . . It was almost a relief to step into the miserable dining-room of the half-way house, even though our appetite was too fastidious to be tempted by the bacon and hominy prepared for the travellers."

The Scot apparently witnessed neither duels nor weddings, for his short report was silent on these subjects. First the jungle, then more recently a wide four-lane highway, took back the spot where he stopped, the old spot where brides became such whether they blushed or not, where their Swamp lords caroused, and the trade in border marriage has long since moved farther down the "indifferent road," down to South Mills, down to Elizabeth City. The urge to elope—to join hurriedly, quietly, in camera—has never gone out of style, and Swamp citizens south of the border have always felt at particular ease with the institution, as William Byrd observed:

"But marriage is reckon'd a lay contract in Carolina, as I said before, and a Country Justice can tie the fatal Knot there, as fast as an Arch-Bishop."

🐊

One lovely July day in 1920 there was a wedding at Arbuckle Landing, the confluence of the Feeder Ditch and the main Canal. Surry Parker, the mustached man who directed Arbuckle Coffee's Stave and Timber Corporation in the Swamp, blew the whistle at the mill there, and several dozen of the hundred black men living and working at the Landing then stopped and stood upon the bluff and from a distance witnessed the union of the bossman's daughter and a newspaperman from the far side of Hampton Roads. From the front porch of the Parker family's home, a Victrola played the Wedding March. Little Jane Parker bore the ring on cedar bark, and the bride walked up and stood before a screen of cypress boughs and said her vows. Thus did Miss Isabel Parker of Juniper Lodge, Arbuckle Landing, Virginia, marry Mister William Harrison of Newport News.

Less than two years before, at Christmastime, 1918, Isabel's younger sisters Elizabeth and Mary Shepard returned from Salem College and Academy to be with their family in Pinetown, the little eastern Carolina settlement where their father had for a quarter of a century manufactured gigantic log-loading equipment for the timber trade. One evening Surry Parker loaded the two girls onto the northbound Norfolk Southern train, and the three of them rode through the night to Northwest, a Virginia whistle-stop just above Moyock, North Carolina. From there they went by car to the mouth of the Feeder, where someone ferried them across the main Canal in a dugout canoe.

Surry Parker was showing his daughters their new home.

"We got there early in the morning," Elizabeth Parker Roberts told me. "Just got out on the land, cause there wasn't any wharf or anything there. Mister Respass had breakfast for us, and he said, 'If I'd of known you all were coming, I would of fisted the biscuits a little bit more.' We just had stools up to a counter, you know. And we just thought that was a wonderful adventure. We liked it."

Eight women surrounded Surry Parker at Juniper Lodge, his wife and five daughters, his mother and his sister-in-law, and it agreed with him just as the Swamp agreed with them all. It was a good thing they took to it, for the Parker family was there until Surry had cut out the Arbuckle tract and they moved on into Norfolk in 1925.

Elizabeth Parker Roberts, tall and erect and clear, looked back across seventy summers and winters with laughter in her eyes and in her voice when she spoke to me of her days as a Great Dismal girl. "We all enjoyed the Swamp, we all did, just loved it. You know, we would maybe see a bear come right up in the cleared space in front of our camp, any old time, snuffling around out there. We didn't go out at night without a light, cause there were so many snakes. Everything was screened, even the chimneys, cause there were so many snakes down there. But right in front of Juniper Lodge, it was all swept, so that you'd see anything that was there. And we'd go up there and sit on the bank, and snakes wouldn't come where there were people talking. We had Delco [a gas generator], which was electric lights. We had lights and running water, hot running water. We had a long room with a big fireplace on one end, and seats on the side of the wall, that had mattresses on them so we could sleep a lot of people. Then in this bedroom, where my aunt and my grandmother stayed, they had two big built-in beds. On this end of the house was our room, the young ladies' room. We had big closets, and bathroom, and two double beds, so we could have company. You know, you had to sleep under a blanket every night in the Swamp, in the hottest summertime, because there was so much shade that it was cool, just really delightful down there. Then Daddy had his room back here, with bricks built all in the wall there in case anybody started shooting, why they wouldn't shoot him! So we were very comfortable down there."

In this dread-named great lonesome place, the Parker girls were cheerful, had fun, felt no sense of isolation at all. They had a piano,

George Dyer's family and home, the Feeder Ditch at Lake Drummond, about 1920

and they had company all the time, girls from the Salem schools come down to encamp with their schoolmates who took such delight in telling folks they were from the Dismal Swamp.

The Parkers had an Oldtown canoe, and a little motorboat, and, for a time, a sea-sled Surry bought from the Navy one time, though for naught, because this last was too powerful for Canal and big-ditch work. But in the other boats the Great Dismal girls took their company from Juniper Lodge back up the Feeder to the Lake, for picnics there at fabled Drummond, for a glimpse, too, of those who then lived at the heart of the Swamp.

They would have seen George Dyer, a light-skinned black man who had been raised for white, taken a black wife named Jane, and moved with her into Edenic splendor as spillway operator for the Lake Drummond Canal and Water Company. Together they populated the spillway colony, with a girl named Jane for her mother, another named Isabel Parker after the woman who had married with a Swamp cypress screen for an altar, a boy John Wallace named for Mister Wallace at the next place on the Canal, and a boy named Lloyd George for the man who had just prosecuted World War I for England.

"In Memory of Whiskey," George Dyer's Feeder Ditch monument to prohibition

Dyer was a cheerful man with an open expression, and, though he worked for the Canal Company, "He kept an eye on the woods for Daddy," Elizabeth Parker Roberts said. She recalled notes that Dyer kept, letters of Swamp observation he regularly sent down the Feeder to the Stave and Timber commandant. He also took Surry Parker in when Parker and another man, lost out near the Lake, made it as best they could for the spillway, the flesh of their legs shredded by the Swamp's ripshin thickets. And there was another thing George Dyer did that undoubtedly pleased Surry Parker, who allowed no whiskey in the camp at Arbuckle Landing and who once kicked a liquor drummer down the Canalbank. When prohibition came to Virginia, Dyer constructed a monument beside a peachtree along his garden path. It was of concrete, stood about three and a half feet tall, with a two gallon earthenware jug atop it, and into the neck of the jug was stuffed—upside down and empty—a liquor bottle, a fifth. At the bottom of the monument was a skull and crossbones, and between the jug and the skull was this legend:

"In Memory of Whiskey, died Nov. 1, 1916, in Va. Long may it remain d. . . . "

Another Dismal denizen back at the spillway, in addition to Dyer and his family, was the man the Parkers knew as Mister Jeffreys, the

Jeffreys, veteran of World War I, "Hotel De Gink.," the Feeder Ditch at Lake Drummond, about 1920

shell-shocked soldier. He was a sad fellow living in a shack ten feet square, with a stovepipe out one side and coon and bobcat hides weathering on the outside wall of the little house. In the seclusion of his Swamp retreat, he posed for Surry Parker, who was always photographing the life of this place. One picture caught him with his carbine in his lap, a small bear draped over his knees, a belt of bullets around his waist; in another he stood before his shack, a sign saying "Hotel De Gink," tacked up above the door and a sheet of Swampwater coming within a stride of his feet. His doughboy uniform made him look sturdy and staunch, but his young and vacant face betrayed it all.

Back at the Landing, the Parkers sat upon a bench overlooking the Canal and watched the world float by: canoes, motorboats, yachts, tugs hauling oil tanks, the double-decked steamer *Emma K.*, whose Captain Snow and black, gold-toothed fireman Arthur Lewis paid twice daily calls at Arbuckle's as the little freightboat plied the waters between Elizabeth City and Norfolk. They watched the *Eloise* and another Arbuckle tug pulling two barges back and forth to the company's mill in South Norfolk, where the Swamp logs became coffee- and sugar-barrel staves. They crossed to the east side of the Canal, by elbow grease and hand-over-hand, on their little eight-person cable-ferry, the *Yuban*, christened such after one of Arbuckle's brands of coffee, and the Parker girls drove frequently into Norfolk with their father, whose office was in the Bank of Commerce there.

If they went in on Fridays, they rode back down into the Dismal not only with Surry Parker, but also with Stave and Timber's entire cash payroll in the car. Elizabeth Parker Roberts remembered literally riding shotgun for her father, a sawed-off twelve-gauge in her lap. One payroll Friday, Surry Parker drove up into someone's yard to put a suspicious hitchhiker out of the car, saying, "Well, get out— this is as far as I'm going!" And the man, outsmarted and foiled, made off into the woods, leaving a club wrapped in a newspaper in the backseat of Parker's car.

"It was dangerous," Mrs. Roberts said. "But Daddy could go down from Norfolk two or three ways, and he varied the way he went. The Green Sea was one, it just had reeds and a road through them."

In Norfolk the girls went shopping, met their father for lunch at the Monticello Hotel, went to see moving pictures and vaudeville shows. They carried crabmeat and roastbeef back home with them, adding these to the wild turkey and venison that various Swamp roamers carried to them at the Landing. "We had bear one time," said Mrs. Roberts, "but I wouldn't advise anybody to eat bear. I think Pap brought us some bearmeat."

Pap Outlaw was the best of the bear hunters, to her recollection. He was a hermit who lived by himself down the road through the Green Sea, in a little house surrounded by pipe-stem reeds, and who took people bear hunting when they wanted to go back in the Swamp. He was a great tall man with coal black hair, part Indian, she thought. Pap posed for Surry Parker with other men and several children and a prize bear, a four-hundred pounder hanging head down from a derrick's loghooks, the engine of Stave and Timber's log train looming behind them all, a little girl in a white frock reluctantly touching the behemoth bruin. "That's Jane," Elizabeth Parker Roberts said, identifying her younger sister. "She didn't much want to put her hand on the bear, but Daddy told her to, so she did."

He was a wonderful shot, but Pap did not entirely confine himself to wildlife. Once he got mad at the engineer of the log train—it was a cardgame argument, or some such—told him he was going home for his gun and coming back to shoot him. The engineer didn't take Pap at his word, and didn't believe the threat until Pap had unloaded several buckshot into him. Surry Parker drove the wounded engineer into Norfolk to get the shot picked out of him, but if Parker had anything to say to Pap about shooting up his staff, Elizabeth Parker Roberts did not recall.

There were hunters and gunmen less fierce than Pap. A party of young men from Petersburg once came down by canoe, planning to bag a bear in the Swamp. After they had failed, Surry Parker offered them an alternative that bailed them out. The Parkers had a small bear chained up near Juniper Lodge, one that had had its foot

Jane Parker and Pap Outlaw hold Pap's big bear's front legs, Arbuckle Landing, Va., about 1920

caught and mangled in a trap, and Parker let the Petersburg boys euthanize the maimed animal and drape it over one of the boats and carry it back to town as if they had met the wilderness and made it their own.

"Brave hunters," I said.

"Weren't they, though?" replied Mrs. Roberts. "They said they'd told that story so much they believed they really had gone into the Swamp and killed that bear!"

Tame times notwithstanding, it was wild and woolly for Surry Parker's five little women over a seven-year span, and they had the sense of having settled the Swamp. Bears on loghooks and on tether, bears snuffling around Juniper Lodge, wild turkey on the table and wild black grapes filling the Canalbank in the fall, snakes in the swept yard there—these were constants of their Great Dismal life. And there was one other that caused their father to construct a water system of canvas pipe back into Stave and Timber's woods: fire. The Parkers lived at Arbuckle Landing long enough to endure most of the great conflagration that swept the Swamp between 1923 and 1926.

Surry Parker, in light vest, and some of his family, touring the eastern Dismal, about 1920

"The woods were just burning, way under, you know, in the peat," she said, "and Daddy told old Uncle Henry—this was getting about suppertime—said, 'Go on in the house and make a fire in the fireplace.' And Henry said, 'Mister Parker, there's plenty of fire in this Swamp, let's don't make any more!' "

There was more to tell, as there always is, before we put a hundred old pictures back into a shirtbox and had done with the Great Dismal for that day: of dead snakes out of the canvas pipes, which Surry made his daughters pose with; of green dust that flew out when the sawblade hit a hollow pocket in a log—someone's long-forgotten money trove—at the South Norfolk mill; of how much prettier she thought it all was back then than now.

"Not everybody would've liked it," I said, before leaving her brick ranch-house in Durham.

"No," said Elizabeth Parker Roberts, looking with such obvious delight and relish back on her seven seasons in the Swamp seven decades ago, "I don't reckon they would."

❧

John Wallace III, a stout bald man in his seventies who lives on the Canalbank a mile and a half north of Arbuckle Landing, was just a little boy when the Parkers moved to Juniper Lodge. But his family had already been three generations on the same ground before Surry Parker and his daughters ever took their first dugout ride across the Canal.

At the corner of Glencoe Street and the Canalbank Highway stands his house, a small dormered cottage that was a store before the Civil War and whose weathered white clapboards cover vertical handhewn juniper planks. From the molding in a high-ceilinged front parlor hang several color paintings: a pastoral of Old World Glencoe, a Scottish farm and château that was this family's ancestral home; a portrait of George Wallace, who built the big two-story Norfolk County Glencoe about 1840, and who, like Faulkner's Sutpen, began to wrest a plantation from an unbridled wilderness; another of John Wallace I, who with his wife turned the storehouse—home of this current John Wallace—into a home and with his father, George, cleared a thousand acres of woods across the Canal and made lumber of the timber in their own sawmill, planted the thousand to corn and sold the cornshucks at harvest to cheap-mattress makers up North, and called the new ground, which dwarfed two-hundred-fifty-acre Glencoe, Dover Farms.

We sat and talked beside a brown spaceheater in a broad den behind the two front side-by-side rooms of the house. On his walls was a wide variety of decoration: a dartboard; a four-foot belt of sleighbells; a rack of green NK and John Deere gimme hats; a picture of his grandfather, John I, in his Confederate uniform with a blue and a green horseshow ribbon on either side of the frame; a photograph of a young brunette next to a small yellow airplane; and, on the mantle, this triptych—two pictures of a young, bonneted woman on a log bridge over a ditch, a third wherein she is joined by a young man. These were the parents of John Wallace III, in the late 1890s, when she was the schoolmarm at the one-room Wallaceton School. Near the three small panels were several Mason jars filled with photochemicals—John III, like his own father, as well as Surry

Swamplands cut and drained for farming, Wallaceton, Va., 1880s

Parker down the Canalbank, had always been fascinated by photography. He has gone so far as to close in a darkroom on one side of his bedroom, the old pre–Civil War store, and has spent years working up a Wallace family tree of color portraiture.

The Wallaces were staple farmers, growers of hay and corn and, in the 1920s and 1930s, soybeans. "Father raised seed soybeans, sold em by mail, most of them, in little canvas bags, up to five pounds, but I've seen em sell as much as a bushel. Some of the strains you've probably never heard of—Carolina, Virginia (that was a small brown bean), Wilson (a little black bean). Then they had one called a Black Eye-brow, looked just almost like the pupil of a person's eye. Mammoth Yellow, Tokyo. Most money I ever made for a bushel of soybeans was on a long-growth bean, pretty sure it came from the Orient, called a Udatan. Fine for soybean hay. Twelve dollars a bushel in 1934."

This family had, earlier and more grandly than any other, practically realized George Washington's dream of Swamp agriculture. They were clearly the right folks to have set themselves up beside the Canal and road, and they were widely known for the breadth of their tillage and industry, even more legendary for their hospitality.

Elizabeth Curtis Wallace, diarist, journalist, and first lady of Glencoe, told the tale of this place before and during the Civil War. Her boys played flute and violin, a kinsman banjo, another bones, and the big house's piano rang out at parties that sometimes played on till dawn. After the War broke out, with two sons in the Army of Virginia and her husband either imprisoned by the Federals in Norfolk or out rambling the countryside doing business, Mrs. Wallace ran the plantation and frequently entertained "unexpected company."

Often this company was Union troops. "Over two hundred cavalry from the 11th Penn. in their retreat from Suffolk have come here and are now encamped upon our farm and their Camp Fires are lighted all around," she wrote on April 13, 1863, adding, "Our soldier has just come in and says they have destroyed all the fodder a great deal of corn and of course they are burning our fence. O the wanton waste they will make of our lumber, produce &c this night." Of another Union visitation she lamented, "Now the Juniper rails will blaze and the fence will fly." On October 22, 1863, Mrs. Wallace reported: "The Yankees are evacuating South Mills and are to establish their line right here at our farm, the N. W. Canal being the line." But six days later she said, "The Guerrillas are growing quite bold now that the enemy has evacuated South Mills and left our neighborhood. One dined with us today." So it went, back and forth. On August 5, 1864, "Lieut. Griswold of the Federals stationed on the Canal came up and tuned the Piano."

Glencoe and Wallaceton were a no-man's-land, and the sense of isolation expressed by Mrs. Wallace in her wartime diaries is painful and bell-clear. "We also hear firing but we can learn nothing, being shut out from all communication with the cities," she wrote in the spring of 1863, and over the twenty months she kept this record, till New Year's Eve, 1864, she frequently ached for lack of word about her sons in the field. In August of 1864 she heard the worst: her son John was wounded in the hip during a counterattack mounted by Mahone's Brigade at the Battle of the Crater, Petersburg, and three weeks later her son William died of wounds received in the Battle of Weldon Railroad.

"Musical tones touch me most tenderly now since he who loved them so has gone. O my son! My William! Must I never on earth hear those dear old flute notes of long ago? Never hear that sweet low humming of 'When the Kye come home,'" she wrote broken-hearted that fall. No amount of Canalbank society could overcome the grief and hardship the War had brought her, and Elizabeth Wallace died in 1866, just fifty years old. Seven years later, over the bitter opposition of his children, George Wallace, sixty-two-year-old widower, married a young woman of eighteen, and then the Wallace children all called their father "1862."

In May of 1888, the Fenian, poet, and Boston editor John Boyle O'Reilly stayed over with the Wallaces. O'Reilly was much impressed by the welcome they extended him, and by the bountiful Dover Farm across the Canal. "The splendid area of fertility was marked in squares of varying color like a map," he wrote, "here the rich dark brown of plowed loam; there the green ridges of early potatoes and corn; yonder a long stretch of clover, and so on until every foot of the fine field was filled with natural wealth." He admired the "enthusiastic earnestness" of these people, and marveled at the Dover Farm drain that ran out through a culvert dug *under* the main Canal and emptied out into Northwest River east of the Canal.

Sixteen years later, Swamp-lover Charles Stansbury met the clan. Coming down from Norfolk on a gasoline launch, the journalist first overshot the estuarine opening to Deep Creek, missing the sign that said merely, "Entrance, Dismal." Then, when the boat took off after tying up for lunch in the Canal south of Deep Creek, a jolt sent a Parker shotgun skidding off the foredeck and into the channel. The boat's engineer dove over and over for the prize gun, retrieving it after an hour, but now Stansbury's party would certainly not make the mouth of the Feeder by sundown. When they came abreast of Glencoe and Dover Farm, here was the Squire of the Swamp in a pith helmet hailing them from shore. The Canal man at Deep Creek had phoned ahead to Captain John Wallace, who now cried out to Stansbury and his crew,

"You're late for dinner! You're late for dinner!"

Nor did the tradition slacken on down through the generations,

Dismal Swamp Canal, looking south, Wallaceton, Va., 1880s

according to the sitting squire, John III. "Why, shucks," he said, "we used to sleep fifteen or eighteen people here a night. They slept all over the place, everywhere. We've had grandmother's wheelchair, I've known em to sit in that and sleep. But everybody was happy and had plenty to eat. Daddy killed sixty hogs a year, for the table. A hundred twenty hams, a hundred twenty shoulders, side meat, bacon, cured here in the smokehouse. It strapped him a lot of times financially, but Daddy set a good table."

But they were just as legendarily inhospitable to the Swamp bears. Captain Wallace, John I, reportedly killed thirty black bears in the winter of 1887–88—one of which he claimed weighed in at 850 pounds—using spring guns set around his cornfields. There were at that time hundreds of wild horned cattle roaming the Swamp, and Captain Wallace more than once heard cattle bellowing in death-battle with bears. John III, who knew and spoke respectfully of the bear-hunting Temples down in Carolina, had bruin-dealings and bragging rights of his own. "I don't know of anybody right off hand that has trapped any more bear than I have. I only trapped the bear to try to keep him out of the field. Thousand-acre farm over there, and he's eating the shirt right off your back when you figure twenty acres of corn each year you're feeding to the bear—that ain't fun!

"And I tried everything I could. Trap one, big steel trap, and kill him and cut him up in pieces and everywhere you see a bear path put a piece of dead bear in the path. That would keep em out about two weeks. After that, it would disintegrate, and the buzzards and the possums would have a feast.

"Best thing we ever had was an electric fence. And that was not foolproof, because when it's real dry and the bear touches the fence, he won't get a shock to speak of. You take when there's some dew on the ground and he touches that wire, he'll have a fit, I can tell you that. I have a friend who was farming over there after I did. He used electric fence, two strands of barb wire a foot and a half and three feet off the ground, running through porcelain insulators on juniper posts. And one had evidently gotten into the field in the early part of the night, and had gone out. He hit that fence on the way out, he knocked, pushed the wire back, tore the fence off of six, eight poles. Tore through the catclaw briars and honeysuckle, went right into there like it was nothing at all, thirty, forty feet back into the Swamp, just like it was a straight hole."

"How many bears did you trap?" I asked him.

"Fifty, seventy-five, maybe a hundred, I don't know. I've caught as high as three of em in a night," he said.

"In the early years, they'd allow you to sell em. And we used to take em, and open em, take their insides out. Then we had ice at the store, and we'd put ice in em, sew em up and put these bears on the *Emma K.*, the freight boat going to Norfolk every day. And they would carry em to what's now a condo, Anheuser Busch in Norfolk, and put em on cold storage there until such time as we had a sale for em. Daddy would contact people in New York, Philadelphia, Baltimore, and there would be a market for these bears. The most I ever got was about thirty-five dollars, but to a young fellow back then, that was big money!"

Farming was not. Though he grew up playing with a small, gray, two-pound tractor, a toy Fordson he was now restoring, and though his family went from mules to tractors when he was a boy, John Wallace III only spent two seasons trying to make a go of it on the Wallace farms. "I lost more money in the second year than I made the first year," he said.

Boats, not beans or corn or even bears, gained his attention and paid his bills. He spent thirty-four years working as a machinist in the Norfolk Naval Shipyard. Nor was he the first of the Wallace planters to go off the farm to make most of his living. His Uncle Will was a marine engineer in Washington, D.C., and his father was in the marine business in Norfolk. John Wallace III remembered some of the boats of his family's life as though they themselves were kin.

There was the sixteen-foot bateau in which his Uncle George used to take the children across the Canal to a sand beach there to teach them to swim, the scow-built boat, four feet wide and of juniper planks, floating like a cork. And, when he was about fifteen, John III's father gave him and his brother an Evinrude boat and motor set, a fourteen-horse Fast Twin. "We had a lot of trouble with it when it was new, but after we got a lot of the bugs out of the thing, it did a Herculean task running up and down Dismal Swamp Canal and into Lake Drummond. I reckon I've been into Lake Drummond more than anybody I know, living right here."

And there were others, special boats his father and uncles had had: a small hand-cranked side-wheeler John II and George had built and used out in the Canal ("Daddy said he always furnished the power, and Uncle George did the steering"); the *Dorothy*, the Wallaces' trim and trig tiny family-size steamboat; and the clan's real marine triumph, the *Tige*.

"That was their showpiece, named for Buster Brown's dog, Tige. Daddy had designed and built this engine, four cylinders, T-head, and it went into this torpedo-boat hull, and she was the fastest thing in Norfolk harbor for many years. They'd say, 'Sic em, Tige!' And the Navy Department ran many a test on her, when she was brand new—she was a guinea pig for a warship. I had the engine taken out when Daddy sold the hull. It was in Glencoe when the big house burned, Thanksgiving Day, 1977. That was a easy starting engine, golly day!"

If vandals haven't gotten at it, he supposed the old T-head still to be in the foundation of the burned-out plantation house, the engine that once fired *Tige* and helped the boat hold Hampton Roads in thrall now idly rusting away, a summer home for wasps, by winter an icy block of metal. Vandals got the single-cylinder, twenty-horse-power Alamo engine that sat out on the Canalbank, the motor that had run the gristmill and cornsheller over on Dover Farm. And fire had engulfed and consumed the Wallaces' great sawmill across the Canal in the fall of 1932.

They had not milled lumber there for forty years, but had stored grain in it, though it leaked at the valleys where the roof sections met, and though its own timbers and pinnings were rotting away. John Wallace III was away at school when fire took the mill, but, though he didn't see it, he heard it told.

"The heat was so terrific, and the wind was in exact line with the durn mill, and brought these piles of burning shingles over—Mama said three and four and five shingles in a piece would come over in a blaze and land on our house and outbuildings. Fortunate for us, there was a large contingency of men about a mile away from here, working on the main road, and they saw the smoke and they came and they got on the roofs of the buildings that were left here, and threw these pieces of burning shingles off. We lost thirteen out-buildings here: outdoor toilets, chickenhouses and corncribs, and Granddaddy's buggyshed and the barn and all that. As Daddy always said, 'That that had insurance on it didn't burn, everything that wasn't insured burned up.' "

A few years later, at the outset of World War II, the federal government took a large part of the Wallace farm beyond the Canal for an airfield. "Which they never completed," said John III. "Completed all the earthworks, but they never did any of the paving of runways." Now, several decades later, these old scars on the land show clearly on the federal orthophotomap of Lake Drummond quadrangle, like some great Phoenician letter, a half mile high, cocked leftward in the cornfield for the eyes of extraterrestrials, and whether to be read as welcome or warning, who knew?

Wallace reckoned that he still controlled some of what he called "the government's land" across the Canal, on account of an old Canal Company promise made his father and uncles, granting them ninety-nine-year use of the far bank because of the Company's failure to replace a Wallace bridge over the Canal after the 1890s rebuilding. But he laughed as he made this reckoning, and he laughed at himself for still farming a little there at Glencoe, with his son John Wallace IV, when he was retired and trying to have none of it, much preferring his photography to his fields.

Outside in the front yard lay a large gray marble slab against a tree. This had once been one of the abutment blocks in a bridge over Northwest Canal, the small waterway that took off from the main Dismal Swamp Canal just a little ways north of where we stood. "We used to take four or five gallon jugs, paddle that juniper bateau down Northwest, get drinking water. Best water on earth."

Across the highway a hundred yards away was the weathered, paintless, two-story house that had long ago been home and head-quarters for the Canal superintendent. "We always called it the Tea House, cause Sister used it for a tea-room back in the Thirties," said John III. I shook hands farewell with one of the precious few men or women in America still living—let alone farming in any way—on the dirt his great-grandparents cleared a century and a half ago, and I strode over to stare at what remained of the Canal-keeper's hall.

Gumtrees grew to the north of the brown house, crepe myrtle to the south, and a dead tree held fast to the Canalbank. There was a riot of honeysuckle everywhere, and vines covered the chimney. Bedsprings leaned against an open, broken window, and an oar on the ground was cracked at the paddle end. The sharp, air-splitting cry of a passing kingfisher turned my head, as it always will, and when I looked back at the Tea House I noticed a tiny crowd of laborers about two-thirds the way up the southwest side. Honey-bees, who measure their generations more quickly and more often than we do, were busy about the clapboard cracks, putting sweet honey into these old worn walls.

🙾

All manner of craft have plied the great Canal, and not all of them have meant to. In mid-October of 1842, one Captain Byard—whose schooner *Leroy* had been lost off Big Kinnakeet, Hatteras Island, North Carolina, a couple weeks earlier—was on his way north on the Canalbank when the horses pulling the stage took fright and pitched the stage, passengers and all, into the Canal. No one was hurt, but poor Captain Byard's books, papers, charts, and maps were the worse for wear.

One odd craft—a seven-hundred-seat theater on a flat-end barge —has the dramatic distinction of having come acropper twice in the Canal. The *James Adams Floating Theatre*, a warm-weather showboat that once toured around the Chesapeake and the Albemarle and lay up winters in Elizabeth City, hit snags and sank in Turner's Cut in November 1929, again elsewhere in the Canal in 1937. So loyal was one old trouper, septuagenarian Pop Neal, that he stayed on stage during the 1929 disaster, never leaving the watery boards once in two weeks, finally stepping ashore when the *Floating Theatre* was raised and righted. On this aquatic venue Edna Ferber spent a week in 1924 doing research for her novel *Show Boat*, the backstage love story that, as a 1927 Broadway musical, inspired Jerome Kern, the show's composer and lyricist, to write the enduring ballad "Ol' Man River."

W. O. Saunders, founder and iconoclastic editor of *The Independent* in Elizabeth City, of whom H. L. Mencken said, "If the South had forty editors like him, its problems would be gone in five years," was driving north on the Canalbank road in late April of 1940 when he suddenly swerved left and went off the road, ran a hundred feet along the shoulder, then vanished beneath the surface of the Canal. The man whose first assignment was covering the sensational 1902 Elizabeth City trial of Jim Wilcox for the mysterious disappearance and death of Beautiful Nell Cropsey carried the secret of Wilcox's private confession to his own death in the Great Dismal Swamp.

Nowadays there is no Halfway House, no big house at Glencoe, no Dover Farm, no shingle flats or juniper barges, no showboat, and the automobiles that ride the rippling road beside the Canal—little more now than a curiosity in the history of American navigation—burn their headlights by day as well as night so drivers might see approaching traffic, to keep them from becoming hypnotized by what all call the monotony of the Canalbank and being drawn into oncoming cars, or off into the switch cane and pines, or worse, like W. O. Saunders, into the dark madeira waters of the old boatway itself.

7

Songbird Swamp

"A paradise for birds—prothonotary warblers were everywhere, threading their way like little yellow shuttles in swift nuptial chase among the dark tree trunks."
—J. J. Murray, 1948

On the first of February, there was ice in the furrows and in the woodland sloughs along the road, and the fields were mists of green, as grassblades insinuated themselves up through stubble and straw. I was on my way to Suffolk, the northwest gateway into the Swamp.

It is an old town, full of late Victorian houses, named for a region in East Anglia where the "south folk" lived. A German surgeon named Schoepf, touring the American Confederation in 1783, passed through Suffolk around Christmastime. He found a town that had had most of its "100 low frame houses" burned by a British raiding party in 1779 and that had been relieved by that party of "a rich booty in tobacco." Schoepf observed small ships in the Nansemond River that were engaged in the West Indian trade—tar, turpentine, pitch, and lumber going for sugar, rum, and coffee. He also complained that "the fine and deep sand in the streets is very incommodious to foot passengers."

Sportsman Alexander Hunter, writing around the turn of this century, said Suffolk was a village of houses set down "higgledy-piggledy style . . . at variance with one another . . . as if each house by settling down where it pleased, and facing where it listeth, north, south, east, or west, was the Fourth of July in itself, and had a vote." The town was full of barrooms, he noted, and those full of east Virginians who drank "nothing in summer but brandy juleps."

While I was stopped at the downtown intersection of Washington and Main, I got a quick dose of dogma before the light turned green. A bumpersticker on the car ahead of me read:

GOD SAID IT
I BELIEVE IT
& THAT SETTLES IT

Down Washington Street I drove on, down this funky avenue of warehouses and black businesses: the Personal Touch Boutique, the Hot Spot Record Shop, Mehalko Makes Bugs Go, the big brick Planters Peanut building, the Duce Pool Parlor, Suffolk Boosters Club, the Frog Hunt Club, Weaver's House of Choice Barber and Beauty Shop, the Horseshoe Cafe, the great long white-brick Nansemond Cold Storage Company, Gold Kist Peanuts, a tiny eatery with 39-cent hamburgers and 49-cent cheeseburgers, and the Feather and Fin Fried Chicken and Seafood.

Two minutes beyond all this enterprise and endeavor, at the heavy, iron-pipe National Wildlife Refuge gate, I met an old-time birdman, ornithologist Brooke Meanley, who has studied wildlife and Southern swamps all his life and who with his wife Anna comes down from the Shenandoah Valley several times a year and wanders his favorite of them all, the Great Dismal. I parked my station wagon and went on into the wilderness with the Meanleys.

▰

Brooke Meanley was a slightly stocky man in his sixties, thoughtful, good-humored, and unhurried. Anna Meanley was small and bright-eyed and, though quiet, seemed as well-versed in the ways of the woods as her husband. They had been good partners for each other, traipsing together about all the Southern bogs and bayous and riverbottoms to which Brooke's work with the Fish and Wildlife Service had sent him.

How had they met? I asked her.

"On a birdwatching trip," she smiled and said.

The day was crisp, not yet fifty degrees, and patches of the snow that had fallen across Virginia earlier in the week lay along the road

Jericho Ditch, mistletoe on high, red bay above switch cane, January 1969

beside Jericho Ditch. As we walked north up Jericho towards the Williamson Ditch, our footfalls noisy on the wet sand road, Brooke spoke easily and steadily about the Swamp world we were moving through.

"There's a pileated woodpecker," he said, when we heard the big bird's cuk-cuk cry. I thought of all the hopeful people who have mistaken pileateds for ivory-bills, and of Audubon's T. Gilbert Pearson, who unsuccessfully sought the ivory-billed woodpecker here in the Dismal nearly a century ago.

"Mistletoe," Brooke pointed up, "a lot of the birds eat that—bluebirds, mockingbirds, cedar waxwings. Red bay, swamp magnolia in here too. This little green vine, that's one of the smilaxes, greenbriar. We've got a lot of the prothonotary warblers, they like the ditches—the number one breeding bird, or nesting bird, in the Swamp. Lot of the birds feed on poison ivy berries. Almost any bird in here that feeds on smilax likes poison ivy berries much better. And the holly berries are a great food, robins love those. That's a red-bellied woodpecker, very common, hear that?

"I think that's a horse-sugar, or sweet pea—good deer foraging plant. Now we're getting into a mesic forest, sort of between swamp and upland forest, lot of white oak in here, and beech. This is a red oak. Swamp chestnut oak, water oak, sweet gum. This north end of the Swamp is drier than the rest of it, an exceptionally dry area compared to the rest of the Swamp. And you get a change. See those pines? These hardwoods, and the loblolly, that means you've got a drier area. Not too dry, cause there's quite a bit of beech right in here, and beech grows where there's a little moisture.

"The pine warblers hang around here. The yellow-throated warbler, which is the earliest warbler to come in from the tropics, comes in here in the middle of March. You usually find them singing in the loblolly pines."

We stopped beneath a tall tulip poplar with a great elbow in one of its upper branches, and Brooke laughed and recalled the classic encounter he had had here. "End of that limb out there is where there used to be a beehive. I was walking down here and I didn't see the bees, I didn't even notice the cavity there. But these bushes were just dripping with honey, and I couldn't figure it out for a while. Then I looked over at the scratch marks, claw marks where a bear had gone up and just pulled out the honey and the comb and everything else—this place was just dripping with it! Little later on I saw the bear a number of times. It was a yearling bear, that sort of had a loafing place in that tree. Big hole, can't see it now, but at that time it was a big opening where he went in. I saw him about half a dozen times—course he'd get out of the way when I'd see him. It's exciting, exciting to see them."

I remembered the story of a surveyor out in the Dismal in the early 1930s, who got some odd and unanticipated excitement from another honey-tree. Maywood Rabey came upon a great cypress, twelve feet in diameter, with a recently defunct bear impaled on a cypress knee, and then he discovered nearby the jungle-twined remains of half a dozen more, all their skeletons with bones broken. There were bees swarming around a hole in a hollow limb high above, and the surveyor realized that these dead bears had slipped, fallen, and died in their quest for honey.

Wandering the Swamp a generation or so ago was a solitary pursuit, said Brooke Meanley, who first came into this wilderness in 1957. "In those days you'd never see anybody in here, except the caretaker, Mister Lynn, would come down occasionally in a jeep, check the water structure, open a gate. Never see a soul. And I'd be in here all day long."

When we started back down Jericho towards Five Points again, I asked him about some borings we had seen in the peat just over a footbridge across the ditch, something about carbon dating.

"Well," he said, "I can't tell you much about that, but it's pretty accurate. I haven't kept up with a lot of peripheral stuff that I should have, but I've read about it. I'm an old-time naturalist."

It was after noon now, and the day had warmed enough for us to unzip our coats. There was a frequent thrumming of small aircraft, our steady footfalls in the wet sand, and tiny ice raining down out of the trees and sounding briskly upon the bushes and vines below like shot.

"The Great Songbird Swamp, I call it," Brooke said. "There're about eighty-five species of breeding birds in here, and it's more of a songbird refuge than anything else. Most of your refuges, or certainly a lot of them, were originally set up as waterfowl sanctuaries. Oh, you get some large waders, like herons, egrets, occasionally along a ditch, a few down at the Lake. Course you get some waterbirds on the Lake, ducks, loons, gulls, not too many. You know, the Lake's pretty sterile. Doesn't have any submerged aquatic vegetation, which is duck food. No emergent vegetation. Just water surrounded by the forest, so it's just more of a resting place for waterbirds."

"What about raptors?" I said.

"Well, you have two basic raptors: the barred owl and the red-shouldered hawk, they're Swamp birds. You get others coming through in migration, few others nest in here sometimes. I've seen a great horned owl in here during nesting season. You get a good migration of hawks across this Lake later on in October: sharp-shinned hawk, Cooper's hawk, broad-winged hawk, and some others. But this is mainly a songbird swamp."

"Why," I finally asked, "is the Dismal your favorite of all the swamps and bottomlands?"

"I don't know. It's an emotional thing, I guess, partly. The fact that it's the northernmost of the great Southern swamps, and all this Southern stuff kind of comes all the way up, is dumped in here. See, these plants are up in here because of the moderating influence of the Gulf Stream offshore. Comes up almost to the Carolina-Virginia line, then it swings over out in the ocean towards England. But I think it's the history of it, the mystery of it, fact that it's the northern limit of so many Southern plants and animals. And it's right next to this huge metropolitan area, a million, maybe several million people. Sort of a special thing, don't you think? To have this area so close to civilization, this great wilderness.

"Plus the fact that one of my favorite birds, the Swainson's warbler, that I've spent more time studying than any other bird, lives in here. In good numbers."

🐊

When he was in the Army during World War II, stationed at Camp Wheeler near Macon, Georgia, Brooke Meanley got to know the Swainson's warbler. In the huge canebrakes of the Ocmulgee River bottomlands he found the bird, and his life's work as well.

The elusive, thicket-loving warbler had scarcely been known of for a century when Brooke Meanley went after it in the coastal plain just below Macon. The Reverend John Bachman discovered the little brown bird when its song fascinated him along the Edisto River south of Charleston, South Carolina, in the early 1830s, and, from Bachman's specimen, Audubon painted it and included it in the 1834 *Birds of America*, naming it for his friend, the English naturalist William Swainson. The real discoverer of Swainson's warbler, though, was apparently Georgia naturalist John Abbot, who came upon it on a tributary of the Savannah River twenty-five years before Bachman's Edisto find. "Swamp Worm-eater," Abbot named it in a note on the reverse of the painting he made of it.

Fewer than ten specimens were taken between Bachman's work and the 1880s, and not until the 1920s and 1930s were ornithologists aware that Swainson's warbler, assumed to be a Coastal Plain bird, was a common breeding bird in the southern Appalachian Mountains. Brooke Meanley has studied this songbird for over forty years, and has written that "although Swainson's is not as abundant as some of the other southern warblers, in 1968 I knew of at least two areas in which I could find 50 individuals in a single day." One of these was the Ocmulgee floodplain, the other was the Great Dismal Swamp, where the first Swainson's warbler captured in Virginia was caught in 1895.

As we first entered the Swamp that February day, Brooke pointed at the small, twiggy cane along Jericho Ditch Lane and said, "Well, we call this 'switch cane.' It's more in the peat soils, whereas the giant cane—the fishingpole cane—it's in the floodplain marsh, whole different soil type. But the switch cane is important here as cover, and the bird specialty of the Swamp, the Swainson's warbler, usually nests about four feet above the ground in the cane, but off a little bit from you, not right along the edge, but back in a hundred, couple hundred feet where there's a lot of cane."

And near the bear honey-tree up north Jericho Ditch he said, "That's pretty good Swainson's warbler territory. Dense, not too dense, but fairly dense, lot of cane. And then there's a lot of sweet pepperbush goes back in there. The cane, the sweet pepperbush, and the greenbriar form most of the understory through an area like this, which is the prime Swainson's warbler habitat."

Seventeen species of warblers fly back from the tropics in the spring and nest in the Great Dismal, and another dozen or more migrate through the Swamp going farther north. Swainson's warbler is the last of the resident warblers to return, arriving here after the middle of April until the first part of May. Their nesting season lasts till late June or early July, and it is during this stretch that the old-time birdman has staked them out, netted and banded them, defined their territories—their individual home grounds.

"Whenever it sings, you go to a spot . . . you just pace all through there, pace maybe to that big tree where you heard it singing. You pace all around them, you plot these points on a map, and after a while you get so many points—you've done it maybe a hundred times—and you get a pretty good idea of the area that it's using, its territorial home range.

"You may be working with a bird for a month, couple months off and on. Come down here, spend three days, come back two, three weeks later, spend three or four more days—all during their nesting period. You usually find the nest, too, at the same time. And you find a nest, you can pretty well nail down the territory. Wherever you hear them singing, then they're on an established territory, and they're defending."

One banded male that Brooke Meanley staked out held down overlapping territories in three succeeding years, areas ranging from 1.6 to 4.8 acres in size. He has watched males with mates start border skirmishes with other males on adjacent territories, bill-clutching and fluttering, a sort of avian wrestling in the air just off the ground.

"They get in conflict. One'll go over there and chase the other. You have your nets here, and when that one comes over here, or both of them come back this way, they hit the nets, they get tangled up and can't get out."

Japanese mist nets are what the bird banders use, very fine mesh nets about ten feet tall and forty feet long with different layers that effectively envelop the birds once they fly into them. Against a background of summer woods, the black netting strung between two metal poles is all but invisible.

"And it's tricky extracting them from the nets, too. Put a metal band on them, you're ready to go," Brooke said.

Once during his many years with this little brown bird, Brooke Meanley found a nest on the east side of Jericho Ditch between Five Points and the fire tower. He could see it clearly from the road, but to get right up to it he would have to cross the ditch on a fallen log. The one he chose was partly sunken, its top about even with the surface of the water, and he thought he was fairly assured of a dunking. So he stripped down to his shorts and walked barefoot and nearly naked across the log to the warbler's nest.

"If you're after something," he said to me, "you'll go on in."

After a time I wondered aloud if he had ever followed the Swainson's warbler to its winter quarters, the Caribbean around 20 degrees north latitude: Cuba, Jamaica, Belize, the Yucatan.

"No," said Brooke, "I've never gone on the wintering grounds. I've wanted to, but I haven't. Could, but I probably won't." The chronicler of wings looked thoughtful.

"Why not?" I said.

"Fear of flying."

☙

Though birdlife was his first love, his interests were catholic, and nothing was too small or slight to escape his careful eye. It was here twenty years ago that he discovered the dwarf trillium, growing scarcely above the leaf litter in the woods of north Jericho Ditch, abloom in late March. Nearby he found another rarity, the wild camellia that blossoms the last week of May.

"Wild camellia is a very small tree, ten or fifteen feet, something like that. And that's in the same family as the extinct *Franklinia*. The third species in that family is a plant that doesn't come quite this far north, called *Gordonia*—loblolly bay is a common name for that. But it is very common in the pocosins of eastern North Carolina. *Stewartia* is the generic name of this tree here.

"Bartram discovered the *Franklinia* down in Georgia along the Altamaha River during the Revolutionary War period—it's never been seen since. Except, he took some slips back to the botanical garden, Philadelphia, so there's some growing in cultivation."

A little later, when he was talking about the nesting habits of the golden mouse, how it will put a roof over an old Swainson's warbler nest and there make its home, he mentioned its Latin name: *Peromyscus nuttalli*. "You've heard of Nuttall, Thomas Nuttall, famous naturalist and botanist way back, Colonial times? All those fellows

Wild, or silky, camellia that blossoms in the Swamp in late May

started around Philadelphia, the latter part of the 1700s, early 1800s, that was the center of early naturalists. Audubon was there. Alexander Wilson, famous ornithologist. Nuttall, the Bartrams, John and William, and a host of others. All lived in Philadelphia."

There was something affecting about the way Brooke Meanley mentioned these men's names, something that bespoke not only a respect for them, but also a strong tie to them, a keen sense of fellowship with them. He spoke fondly, too, of an old National Museum naturalist he had known when he worked at the Smithsonian, before he went with the Interior Department, a man named Paul Bartsch who had come into the Swamp in June of 1897 and June of 1899, and spent a week each time in the white rough-board hotel at the mouth of Jericho Ditch into Drummond, touring the Lake taking specimens of birds and mammals with a .22 pistol.

"He found a lot of bats nesting in those big old cypress trees out in the Lake," Brooke said. "Something else I remember: we were out at Doctor Bartsch's place on Pohick Creek—that's a tributary of the Potomac, near Mount Vernon—a bunch of us one time, and we found a Bachman's warbler, rare bird, right near his house, but he was too old, too weak, to come out and see it. It was kind of sad."

A sad thought, indeed, and a very real concern for Brooke Meanley, who in 1986 was in an auto wreck and, in a separate incident in Beaufort, North Carolina, while staying in an inn and going out by day to study the Croatan woodlands, broke both his knees in a fall down a stairwell. The birdman knows well that he cannot forever go down into his beloved swamps and bogs and pocosins. What else has he seen, does he remember from all his days in the Great Dismal?

He recalls the dark-leaved cross vine creeping up the trunks of tall timber, likewise the climbing hydrangea, both vines at or near their northern limit. And he recalls the otters that go sleek and fleet in the ditches below, one otter in particular that he once watched working underwater, leaving a line of bubbles for him to trail it by, and bringing crayfish back to its two near-grown pups, waiting with their heads just out of their den on North Jericho Ditch. And he recalls the snakes of the Swamp.

"Well, you don't see many snakes. There're a lot of snakes here, but you don't see them. I've been here for a week at a time without seeing a single snake. But you have the canebrake rattler, the copperhead, and the cottonmouth—the three poisonous snakes. The copperhead's the most abundant of the three, and the canebrake rattler and the moccasin are at their northern limit right in this general area."

I reminded him of the popular impression of the Swamp as a snake-infested morass, and the oft-repeated tales and warnings about snakes dropping like ambushers from trees and cane into boats passing beneath.

"Yeah," he laughed, "that's fable. The thing about the poisonous snakes, the one *good* thing about them, they're sluggish, much slower than the nonpoisonous snakes. The snake you see the most is the black snake, which is harmless. Man, they can take off! Very quick, very fast! But you don't see many snakes wandering around here all day long, middle of summer."

Once, walking, Brooke and Anna and I stopped and studied some tracks in the road along Jericho. "This looks like a bobcat, very much like a bobcat, fairly fresh. You hardly ever see a bobcat, but you do see the bear." Then he stood still a moment, and wondered and worried over the fate of bear in the Great Dismal.

"You're not allowed to shoot bears in the Swamp, but they go around the edges, and a hunter will come on one sometimes and shoot him. I think the Virginia game man in charge of this section told me they killed nineteen around here this year. The farmers get a permit, bear goes out in his cornfield, they shoot him. Some are going to be killed by automobiles, not too many, a few.

"This friend of ours, the mammalogist Don Schwab, has a collection now of forty skulls of bears taken here or right around the Swamp, killed by automobiles, hunters, farmers, and this is just in the last three or four years he's collected these. Right north of here, up in Magnolia, a village up above the Swamp, someone had some beehives. A bear was getting into the beehives, and he got a permit and shot that one.

"So they keep picking away at them."

⬅

Just before sunup one frigid January morning years ago, along east Corapeake Ditch, Brooke Meanley watched line upon line of robins flying out of their roost in the evergreen shrub bog. The Swamp was covered with snow, a very light frosting, and during the day he saw thousands of the birds feeding on gallberries, or inkberries.

One million robins, he estimated, the most he has ever seen in the Great Dismal.

They are common here, if not in such magnificent numbers. At the Wildlife Refuge headquarters on Desert Road, former manager Jim Oland has watched clouds of robins fly over for an hour at a time. And Brooke and Anna and I saw some in a wintertime band of birds working the woods of Washington Ditch.

"They're not a member of the regular band, usually," Brooke said. "But birds attract birds, that's what it's about, and the bands are a stable thing in the wintertime. It's real interesting in the fall, these bands begin forming. Then the warblers, fifteen or twenty species, and some of the other birds from the North start coming through—they'll join these bands too. And it's the Carolina chickadee and the tufted titmouse that are the key birds holding this band together, because of their constant calling. Robins are hanging by themselves most of the time, though."

Or almost by themselves. Robins often roost with blackbirds, the old-time birdman said, but not in the same section of the roost. If the robins go to roost first, blackbirds sometimes displace them—and it is the blackbird that was the subject of Brooke Meanley's most astounding avian activity in the Great Dismal.

Twenty-five years ago, farmers after pulling the vines from the ground were still putting their peanuts up in shocks to dry. These big brown mounds, ten or twelve feet high and nearly as broad and with a central stake round which they were wound protruding from the top, were everywhere in the Down East fields. And in the fall, great swarms of blackbirds—redwings, grackles, cowbirds, and starlings—were coming out of an enormous Swamp roost that straddled the Virginia and Carolina line at east Corapeake Ditch, and they were tearing up the peanut shocks there in the fields.

Several students from Virginia Polytechnic Institute, working with monies granted them by the Fish and Wildlife Service, set about solving the blackbird-peanut problem, and Brooke Meanley occasionally came down from Patuxent Wildlife Research Center to help them. How many birds were they up against? they needed to know. The blackbirds would return to roost nightly along the same flightlines, and Brooke and his fellows positioned themselves with large-negative aerial cameras and took big pictures from which they could count this fabulous flock:

Thirty million blackbirds.

Fish and Wildlife had had success trapping blackbirds in Arkansas with a light-trap, a huge tunnel of netting forty feet tall and a hundred wide at its mouth, funneling down to a small tent with several thousand-watt lights inside to attract the birds from the roost at night. One night's catch of starlings and blackbirds was 120,000, and Brooke Meanley's team decided to try the light-trap technique in the Great Dismal.

By day they worked cutting lanes in the dense shrub cover, hundred-yard trails that fanned out from the mouth of the net. A cousin of one of the workers paid the team a visit one day, crawled into a tent where the floodlights were stored to take a nap, and got a visitor of his own. When the lanecutters returned, they discovered beartracks all around the tent—the cousin had slept right through it.

Once the trails were cut and the netting strung, ten or twelve men would go out in the Dismal dark to the end of the lanes and attempt to herd the roosting birds into the trap once the floodlights were turned on. All those millions of birds were in that pocosin, but they were all spread out. The beaters coming down the lanes awakened and impelled very few to their doom, and the low density of the great roost was defeating the operation.

"That's when we went after the helicopter," Brooke told me.

"See, all the fellows had given up and gone home except two of us, a V.P.I. boy and myself. My partner, Joe Hardy, went to the Elizabeth City Coast Guard Station and talked them into having a helicopter pilot take Joe over to the roost to try to herd the birds. They flew up above Highway 17, then cut into the Swamp when they saw the light beam I pointed up towards the sky, then flew around above the roost for about an hour—and *still* no birds to speak of came into the trap."

"Was the propwash supposed to blow them into the trap?" I asked.

"No, we thought the headlights would push them in there, and the noise. But there was a light on the underside of the helicopter that was directed towards the ground. The blackbirds were attracted to that light and were flying up and hitting the belly of the copter. The pilot was afraid his communications might be knocked out, so he got *another* helicopter to come up from Elizabeth City. Now two helicopters—one behind the other—tried for another hour or so.

"Still didn't catch any birds."

❧

In August we went back into the Swamp together, and Brooke said the water was about as low as he had ever seen it. Just below Five Points there was a big outbreak of sweet pepperbush, abloom with little white flowers and growing into the ditch, and partridge pea and the red-stemmed Hercules'-club (bear food, Brooke said of it) were along the road there too.

We spooked a green heron, and watched it moving about in the Swamp, its yellow legs standing out against the green jungle. We heard a white-eyed vireo, and a cuckoo—the rain crow. Down Jericho Ditch the road doglegs across the ditch, and there near the brick-rubble in the woods we saw an Acadian flycatcher.

"It often nests over the road," Brooke said. "They like an opening, they fly out and catch stuff. It's easier out over the road than it is in the Swamp."

I had my old friends Jake Mills and Tommy Thompson along on this outing, and Tommy focused on the birds while Jake remarked upon the Swamp's "odor of eternal rot." It had rained a good deal in the past twenty-four hours, and butterflies and dragonflies crowded the mudpuddles in the road. By midday the Swamp was steamy and fetid again.

We followed the Meanleys back out of the Swamp and on south to Washington Ditch and into the Lake. Morning glories, pink and purple, wound around corn in the fields, and down Washington Ditch there was much pokeweed and orange and yellow jewelweed along the ditchbank. The ditch was extremely muddy, and there was trumpet vine hanging beyond the waters, locusts grinding out across the way.

Lake Drummond was so low there was a sandy beach on the north side, and Tommy and I walked around looking at bolts, nails, pieces of plates, and linoleum, all of which were scattered about the Lake-bottom shallows where a hunt cabin or two had been. "I woke up on the edge of Lake Drummond in the middle of the Dismal Swamp," Tommy had written in his 1984 play, *The Last Song of John Proffit*, adding, "I can't tell you how I got there, but it's a hell of a

Open water in the southwestern Dismal, a tributary swamp one mile east of Corapeake, N.C., 1880s

place to wake up." Now at high noon he was seeing the real thing for the first time.

One of the Refuge rangers told us the Swamp was so dry that not only was a lightning-set fire burning over on the west side of the Lake, but also that a small aircraft had come down into Drummond and landed on that northern beach.

"Who was fool enough to pull that?" I asked.

"We never knew. Never saw the plane," he said. "Just saw the tiretracks in the sand."

Cycles of the ocean's elevation and subsidence created the collection of ancient seabeaches underlying the Lake, the peat, all of this Swamp, that has its own, far shorter, cycles of wet and dry. Not too many years ago, firefighters extinguished a lightning blaze burning only two hundred yards from the Lake's edge with water that had to be brought in from outside the Swamp, so dry was Drummond.

One winter's day, when Brooke and I talked about the question of the Swamp's drying out, he said that he just could not tell, by his eye, whether it was or not.

"Come down here in the spring sometime, maybe March, and it'll be dry. Come down next March, and it's full of water, so you can't tell that way. Only the hydrologists can answer that question." Not much later that same day we stopped at a turn in the road, near the head of Washington Ditch, where Brooke thought he saw a little activity. He quickly spotted a myrtle warbler—"A hearty warbler that winters here"—and a hermit thrush. And then he turned back to our earlier talk, saying, "You know, a lot of folks, when I show them a bird list of the Swamp, are very surprised to see the ovenbird so high on the list. Because it's a bird that likes upland woods, a lot of leaf mantle, and a dry ground cover.

"So maybe the ovenbird being so common, that's enough to tell you that the Swamp really *is* drying out."

⮌

Late in a February day we rambled down into North Carolina to see the largest cypress Brooke had ever encountered in the Great Dismal. The tree grew about a hundred yards into the Swamp, just south of U.S. 158 at the boundary between Pasquotank and Gates Counties. It was about six feet in diameter, with huge two- and three-foot bulbous knees all around it, extending to as far as forty feet from the tree itself.

We flushed the same woodcock twice as we stomped through the switch cane going in, and a third time after I tripped and fell over a half-submerged barbed-wire fence. Then we went nearly a mile west, back into Gates County, to look for catbirds in a long jasmine and greenbriar hedge on Weyerhauser Ditch.

Before we had gotten very far, two hunters in a pickup truck drove in past us, parked, and let their rabbit dogs out. Seven beagles started yelping and working a viny thicket where two roads came together at an angle, and the hunters thrashed about noisily at the edge of the thicket. The Meanleys and I moved steadily south down Weyerhauser Ditch, a good half mile below the hunt.

The last fall's hurricane had left a good many windfalls all over the Swamp, and I highstepped through a bramble to a broken

Bald cypress, 125 feet tall and four or five hundred years old, southern Dismal (N.C.), in the 1970s

juniper, wresting a piece loose from the trunk's sharp stalactite splinters—it smelled cedar clean, like all the very old beach cottages I remembered from my young days down at Nags Head and Kitty Hawk.

We turned two corners and headed back for our cars. No birds were moving, and the Meanleys thought we had seen about all we were going to see.

"Ah, yeayeayea yea yea yea yea!" one of the rabbit hunters cried, exhorting his dogs, his calls carrying up the road to us on the wind that had risen. "Whee! Whis, whis, whis!"

When we were about forty yards from the hunter, and walking towards him, the rabbit finally flushed—midway between us and the man with the shotgun—and ran our way. The hunter raised his twelve-gauge about halfway before he saw us, and his disappointment was evident in his dropped shoulders. He lowered the shotgun and called gamely our way:

"Don't worry, I wadn't gon shoot you."

It was our long day's end in the Great Songbird Swamp, and if the hunters ever got another chance at their prey, we were never to know. Back out at the highway, the Meanleys and I wished each other well and parted company and drove our separate ways west. It does me good whenever I think of them, at one with each other and with the great wilderness, their hearts filled with the melodies of these big boggy woods.

8

The Great Dismal

"I can fancy that it would be luxury to stand up to one's chin in some retired swamp a whole summer day, scenting the wild honeysuckle and bilberry blows, and lulled by the minstrelsy of gnats and mosquitoes!"—Henry David Thoreau, *A Week on the Concord and Merrimack Rivers*, 1849

"Everything changes," Reggie Gregory said.

We were sitting in hobbled chairs out in his tractor shed at Tadmore, the fog-enshrouded wilderness wall just beyond us, the wet air of the November afternoon full of mist one minute, roaring with winter rain the next. Hurricane Kate had just blown up through Apalachicola and Georgia, flooding full the creeks and swamps and pocosins of eastern North Carolina. Seagulls were stark chalk-white against green winter cover in the fields, cotton remnants where stubble stood were drooping gray and dripping wet, and more than a few men were afield with shotguns in all this wet weather.

Reggie was speculating about whether or not the Dismal Swamp Canal along U.S. 17 would stay open, shrugging over its prospects. But what he was really concerned about, and feeling very deeply, was how much the Swamp he had known and ranged all his life was now changed forever, not just cut over, but *preserved*. The Swamp was saved, but because this meant his progeny could never hunt and trap it as he had, in a way Reggie felt the Great Dismal was almost lost to him.

Though he was the park ranger for the Dismal Swamp State Park—fourteen thousand acres bounded by Bull Boulevard on the south, Forest Line Ditch on the west, the state line to the north, and the Canal on the east—his dealings with people in government, whether state or federal, mystified him. He was playing a role that no one had really written, only titled.

"I bout have no contact with the State," he told me. "They give me that old four-wheel-drive, but it rides so rough I'd rather use my own truck, even if I have to put my own gas in it. I don't write them, don't call em, nothing. Never hear from them.

"Oh, the new man from Raleigh came to see me. I asked him what had happened to the other fellow. He said, 'Oh, he's gone now. I've taken his place.' I said, 'Well, good—I didn't like him worth a damn.' Course I didn't mean it, I was just sayin that. And that was the only time I saw this new guy. I don't have nothing to do with them folks up in Raleigh, cept I get a paycheck from em, and I go back in the Swamp, and check on it, see that it's still there."

The old man leaned back and his chair creaked and the woodstove he had built breathed with a slow and steady insuck of air as it burned away on wood he had cut and split. On the refrigerator in the corner was a brunette in a revealing macrame bathing suit—"Navy boy put that up, fellow who was rebuilding his truck in my shop here," Reggie said. On the shedwalls were hoses, cords, funnels, headgaskets, on the floor a small ballpeen hammer. Beyond a bandsaw and a drillpress was a new bulldozer trailer he was welding together, not yet finished but not far from it. He said he had gotten new orders not to maintain the roads and ditchbanks in the state park with his bulldozer and brushhog, but from now on only with a chainsaw and an axe the state would stake him. "Won't be no road, if that's the way they expect me to keep it up," he said, ever mystified.

North Carolina had a treasure in its park here, he thought, a set of jewels no one knew what to do with. Reggie thought the state should cut out a juniper thicket, take the money and put a campground over on the Canal by U.S. 17, and make it possible for people to come into the Carolina Swamp and stay awhile and get to know it. He was made head to toe of peat and juniper and Swampwater, and he had an ingrained contempt for those in power who assessed his home grounds from afar or who came in sporadically and at best gave the territory a few minutes of cursory windshield appraisal.

"The state's got a juniper thicket right there on the Forest Line Road, right side, worth a million dollars today, that one thicket.

Damn fools want to give it to the Interior crowd. Would of done it hadn't been for me—I went to see this guy over there in Bertie, Monk Harrington, told him what they was getting ready to do, and he and Melvin Daniels blocked it. I think that's the reason they got pissed off at me, they knew I'd done it. It didn't make any sense to me. Just gon give it to them."

So it came to light that Reggie had run afoul of some bureaucrat or politician, and someone was trying to clip the old Swamper's wings: telling him to clear the jungle's roads with the meanest of tools; upbraiding him about his taking an occasional deer from the Swamp, hunting for which he said he had had express permission; and ordering him to clear his any and every action in the Swamp with another warden in a nearby park. It all made him mad, and sad, at once. No title, no redrafted job description would have made him one whit more or less proprietary about his place in the world, his Swamp, than his very birthright had made him. He said:

"One of the head men out of the Raleigh office a year or two ago was down here riding with me and we was riding with the head man of the Interior up here, going right down Corapeake Road, and of course all that road belongs to us, the park, and he said,

" 'Reggie, we just as well give them this road, hadn't we?' And I said,

" 'Sir?' And he said,

" 'Don't you think we just as well give them this road, cause, hell, we own both sides of the road?' I said,

" 'If you gon give em this road, why not give em the whole damn park, just as well, cause we ain't gon have a thing left if you do!' And the Interior man he just laughed.

"We got some of the dumbest bastards in the world running this state."

The mistshroud and the storm were so socked in that it was nearly dark by half past three. For a spell then it rained steadily and more heavily, and had it not been November and I not known better I might have taken the loud battering on the tin roof above us for hail. It was hard to hear, but Reggie did not raise his voice except for occasional emphasis. We had been sitting there without rising by now for nearly three hours, and we had entered a new moment.

There was something sterling in the emotional air, some melding of Reggie Gregory's fierce integrity and the overscoring storm outside.

It was a high and affecting sadness, and I struggled to follow the muffled voice that articulated it as Reggie drew more deeply into his own soul for the things he said next, as he drew upon the wells of that sadness and grew tearful.

"Excuse me if I get a little sentimental sometimes. That old Swamp is my home, my living, my life. Now they gon take it away from me. And all I ever worked for and enjoyed, my grandson won't ever be able to go in there and enjoy it, what I did, and that's what tees me off. Just on account of some screwball, that don't know no more about this Dismal Swamp than I know about Washington, D.C., and ain't never been here."

From his rear pocket he pulled a handkerchief, wiped his eyes and his nose and shook his head, and then recalled for me and for himself too another man, another loss, and music that came to us in the shed across the distance of a half a century.

"There was a colored fellow named Holly, drove the Cedar Works train in the Swamp way back. And he had a son that worked with him, was the brakeman. And there was two logs, just like that out over the ends of the flatcars, and one day the son, coupling up the cars, he backed up and them logs came together on him, mashed him, killed him. And it like to ruined Holly. And when he'd go out, years after that when they come on south through the Swamp, on through here, see, our field, Papa's field, joined that railroad. He'd come right by with that trainload of cars, and that old fellow could blow the whistle in there, and late evenings when he'd come out, every day, he would blow that steamwhistle in the engine and play 'Nearer, My God, to Thee.' Pretty as anything I ever heard in my life.

"Couldn't help from crying sometimes."

🐢

One fall fifteen years before Reggie Gregory was born, a young poet stood on a boardinghouse porch in Canton, Massachusetts, knocked on the door, and waited to see the love of his life. He knew she was not expecting him, but he was dressed up in a new suit the girl's own mother had bought for him, and he bore with him two slender books of poetry he had written for his love. He was twenty years old, there in all earnestness—surely she would see him.

Surely she would not. He had surprised her by riding the train all night from Lawrence to Canton and presenting himself so. The girl refused to entertain him there at the boardinghouse, or anywhere else in town. What of the gift of his heart? He showed her the identical small volumes of verse, the entire edition of his five-poem collection, and offered one to her. Each of them was to keep and cherish a copy, like halves of a heart locket or, better still, like wedding rings.

She looked at the little brown book he held out to her, its name "Twilight" stamped in gold foil onto the dark pebbly leather, took it from him as if she had been delivered no more than a newspaper or a prescription, and shut the door where he stood as she disappeared into the house.

Robert Frost was crushed.

He wandered down the railroad tracks, tore his half of the covenant of love into shreds, and scattered these remains along the roadbed of the train. All that was left to do was to destroy himself.

On Election Day, 1894, young Frost set out, traveling by train from Lawrence to North Station, Boston, from South Station there to New York City, then by steamer south to Norfolk, Virginia, where he disembarked the next morning. After he had had breakfast—all he would eat that day—he asked the way to the Dismal Swamp.

Now he was on foot, dressed only in light clothing and a thin topcoat, and it was the end of the day before he reached Deep Creek, sundown before he saw the Canal. The moon was nearly full, and Frost, fearful since childhood of the dark, trudged along towards the wilderness, stopping to lighten his grip by pitching out some clothes and a couple of books.

Brambles and forest enclosed the road, tunneling it after a while. The mudhole quagmire he walked down soon sank beneath a shallow sheet of water, and now the poet strode upon a plank walk perhaps a foot above the water. What would he do? Dive in and drown in the cold waters of the Canal? Make his way by swimming, by boat, to the western side and walk off into the Big Swamp, there to lie weak and starving up against some gumtree none save he had ever seen? Or would the enormous black man with a shouldered axe that Frost fancied he sensed hard on his heels finally lop off his head?

If Robert Frost had in mind a poem of his own death, some epitaph short or long that might form and play in his head as he sank into the mire, he did not write it here in the Great Dismal. Somewhere between Deep Creek and the old Northwest Lock ten miles to the south, it must have dawned on him that his romantic suicide would have no effect on its intended audience, Miss Elinor White, if his body were never found and neither she nor anyone else ever heard about it.

At Northwest Lock about midnight that night, he boarded a small steamer bound for Elizabeth City, where it lay docked for most of the next day awaiting a party of duck hunters. They were boisterous, well-provisioned, liquor-swilling, and they swept him along with them for a night and a day of it down at the old Nags Head Hotel.

"I was trying to throw my life away," he repeatedly told Lawrance Thompson, his biographer, but instead he walked and boated right through the Great Dismal, and, now, Robert Frost's Swamp adventure was over.

In time he would win the two things the want of which had driven him towards the Dismal and death: Miss White and the world's respect for him as a writer. And in our time his few lines about the bird that is now so populous in the drier Great Dismal stand as an elegy to the great cypress and juniper Swamp, the wet Desert, that once was.

The Oven Bird

There is a singer everyone has heard,
Loud, a mid-summer and a mid-wood bird,
Who makes the solid tree trunks sound again.
He says that leaves are old and that for flowers
Mid-summer is to spring as one to ten.
He says the early petal-fall is past
When pear and cherry bloom went down in showers

On sunny days a moment overcast;
And comes that other fall we name the fall.
He says the highway dust is over all.
The bird would cease and be as other birds
But that he knows in singing not to sing.
The question that he frames in all but words
Is what to make of a diminished thing.

❧

The hunt camps on stilts, the cabins on the shore, are all gone from Lake Drummond now, all except a weathered hut on the southwest shore stove in by a huge gumtree, the tan-and-brown shanty at the mouth of Jericho that the Refuge may soon remove, and the gray house a few hundred yards to Jericho's east that lies sunk to its ceiling, so only attic and roof and eaves protrude from the Lake. Wasps buzz around the tin roof of the sunken ruin, and gable-boards creak and sway loose to the rhythms of the winds and waters.

Jake Mills and his boy Mark and I had gone into the Lake for a spell of fishing in early May of 1987, and though we caught nothing in the Lake larger than a potato chip, it was a fine, cool weekend, a grand time to tour the old Lake and see the remains of hunt habitation along its marge. As we had headed up the Feeder on a Friday afternoon in our seven-and-a-half-horse johnboat, a couple of bikers espied our boatload of goods—blue-and-white-striped canvas tent, beat-up Coleman stove, red coolers and green—and one of them said:

"Y'all going camping?"

"Yeah," Jake said.

"Takes a lot of stuff to go camping, don't it?"

"Yeah," Jake said again, now sensing that we were being cased and adding, "but it's just a bunch of junk, though, really."

At midnight that night we went out upon the Lake, and it was cool and clear. I studied the treeline pattern where the Feeder came out, so that we might find our way back into the little notch through the woods and not spend all that cold night cruising the shore. Back at

Swamp magnolia, abloom in the Dismal in May

the spillway when we returned, there were many low mists playing rapidly across the water.

Saturday morning we were back out on the Lake just past ten. There had been pollen in sheets all over the Feeder Ditch going out, and we had slowed to study the hunter's camp on the north shore of the Feeder just west of the spillway—a log cabin with a hundred A-1 sauces propped in the kitchen window, deer antlers all along the outside wall, big longhorn steerhorns at an upstairs window, a dog-pen big enough for a dozen hounds.

Songbirds were everywhere singing out to beat the band. Blackbirds swarmed in a hollow gum along the southeast shore, its top blown totally out. We saw mallards, kept flushing a great blue heron that would fly ahead of us, settle, then take off again at our approach.

These ruins lay about the Lake: a privy on the north shore, tilting over at a sixty degree angle, an ornate wrought iron rail pitched off into the woods, a corrugated tin building that looked like a pair of pony stalls, an upended kitchen sink and a hotwater heater in the water, matrices of charred pilings here and there in the shorewaters where hunt clubs had obeyed the federal order to remove their camps by burning them where they stood, a bike reflector on a gumtree, and a chipped chamberpot tied to a tree with a red bandana.

Our fishing was far better back at the spillway Saturday afternoon, where ten gates were open and spilling. Jake and Mark pulled in ten catfish and a couple of perch, and were happily frying them up for our big Swamp souse-down when one of a group of fey, urban campers happened by and said,

"What're you fixing there?"

"Catfish," Jake said.

"*Catfish*?!" the man said, horrified. "You mean you're going to eat *catfish*?"

"That's right," said Jake, defiantly flipping one and splattering grease, "catfish."

The spillway spit was filthy with caterpillar worms and toads that night, but these had secreted themselves away by the time I awoke next morning to the cries of a kingfisher strafing the Feeder Ditch. I wandered off into the big trees and tangles past an old sluice near the boat railroad, tracking for fifteen minutes or so a rufous-sided towhee. Then we fried bacon and scrambled eggs and ate up and cleared out, listening as we loaded and moved slowly down the ditch to the urban men, who having polished off a couple of boxes of Suzanne's Danishes now suspected fellow campers of stealing their cache of deli roastbeef and were sounding off about it, shrill and petulant in their designer-labeled camp outfits.

When we were out of earshot, Jake said of them and their complaint: "You were talking about diminishment here in the Swamp? Well, there it is! There it is."

A little ways more down the Feeder, we cut the engine and flipped a huge dead belly-up snapping turtle with one of our aluminum tent stakes, admired its claws that could easily strip the flesh from a deer, or a man. Through the cooter there was some purchase on the primeval Swamp whence it came, and we were still speaking of it— granting it the honor due a lion of the ancien régime, like Sir Walter Ralegh, the Last Elizabethan, at his beheading—as we passed the

Young great horned owl, edge of the Great Dismal

Bongo Club and Blind Man Road outside South Mills and entered the Swamp again beyond Tadmore, where buttercups by the billion were putting forth.

🐝

The Lake is pink-rimmed in spring, when all the maple in the marge of the morass puts forth like cherry, and the cypress that still stand in the shallows are the lightest and most feathery green. Fetter-bush hangs abloom at the mouth of Jericho Ditch, bullfrogs ga-lunk there where the Lake just slides off into the Swamp, and thrushes sing their looping, liquid songs. Standing up on the ditch-banks to be counted are fronds and fiddleheads, for ferns are in near riot here—cinnamons, royals, sensitives, Virginia, and narrow chains, thirty species in all, with even the rare log fern presenting itself nowhere more than in the Dismal. The whole jungle swarms over itself in remarkable convolutions of fecundity, yellow and black butterflies and dragonflies and lavender moths alighting everywhere, slow-croaking frogs in the musky sloughs of North Jericho Ditch, grapevines leafing out where they twine upon holly, Swamp magnolia blossoms coming on, pollen swirled thickly in the still dark waters of the ditches, and everywhere hanging over and falling into these little canals the heady yellow jasmine sweet-scenting the air.

I was staring at an eight-foot wild azalea way up Jericho one bright late April day, its white flowers tinged with pink, when a female wood duck with six ducklings came paddling down the ditch. When she saw me she squealed and went off to the north, dragging her left wing and playing sick-bird, while the six little ones kept on downstream, stepped up their paddle-pace, and ducked under the lowest hanging branches till I moved along. Warblers were singing, mourning doves too, and a pileated woodpecker crying out from somewhere east of Jericho Ditch finally went lope-flying across the road and dropped down into a thicket from which three great, thick-barked pines loomed up and towered over all.

A big beautiful maple at the confluence of Jericho and Williamson Ditches was a huge pink ball, its flight-seeds still hanging all a-cluster. I had picked up a shotgun shell from the road, a Charles Daly 12, and was idly turning it in my hand when I heard the deep varinoted horn of a diesel engine. The long train went rumbling through the Swamp over the ancient roadbed, setting up a strong drumming rhythm of the rails that went on and on till I thought what an awfully long train this was, and how much its rocking rhythm now reminded me of the highspirited, highstepping black marching band from P. W. Moore High School in Elizabeth City when I was a boy, the beat going:

BUM bu DUM bum
BUM bu DUM bum
BUM bu DUM bum
Bu-bu-bu-BUMP!

After a few minutes I realized that the freight train was miles west of the Swamp, and what I had been listening to for some time now was another marching band, this one working out on the playing

field of John F. Kennedy High School in Suffolk, snug up against
the northwest corner of the Swamp. The drumming of train and
band had been so well conjoined that, but for the syncopation of the
musicians, I might well have imagined the train to be ten or twenty
miles long.

A hundred thirty-five years before, early in the Civil War, Virginia's William Mahone played shrewdly and well upon the imagina-
tion of the Federal commander of Gosport Navy Yard. Mahone, who
had built one of the rail-lines through the northern Swamp, ordered
his engineer to move slowly, easterly, towards Gosport, blowing his
whistle long and often. Aware that the Gosport commandant had
intelligence Lee might be advancing on Norfolk, Mahone counted
on this theatrical military play—echoing train-rumbles and steam-
shrieks—to convince the Federals that Southern soldiers were rail-
ing in on them. The Federals fled the mock attack, and Gosport fell
bloodlessly, if briefly, to the South.

I stood at that pink-maple corner in the Great Dismal and
thought of the freight train I had just heard, how it had rumbled
slowly over Mahone's old roadbed, the causeway of Swamp earth
packed upon a never-rotting cypress corduroy, a roadbed so fine that
the president of Norfolk and Western could say in 1949 that it
"requires astonishingly little maintenance." And at that moment too,
I had not only the strongest sense of the history of this place, but also
the stern feeling that history here was finished.

Nothing more will happen here, I thought. Just the endless leaf
going down to leaf, the cold gray winter when waters from the west
recharge the peat muck and mire, the hyperfecundity of the jungle
in spring, the yellow flies of July and August, high summer's curse of
the Swamp. Scientists will descend on Great Dismal till in time
perhaps the Swamp will have been studied to the death of its mystery. Perhaps. But as I mused on Mahone that late April morning,
his track-clattering trains, his successful gambit against Gosport for
the Confederacy, I thought too: gone are the Nansemonds, and
whatever other Indians named or no who used God's own smokehouse, this Swamp, as their own; gone are the shinglegetters, and all
the armies phantom or real of runaway slaves; gone too the legions
of lumbermen who ran the narrow-gauge rails into the most remote

reaches of the Swamp and in our time, or our fathers', tore down the rest of the cypress and juniper in the thousand-year-old woods and sent it out into the world as lifeboats for the Coast Guard and cedar shakes for cottages all over the East and South and as barrels to bring back coffee from Colombia far away.

Now there were only a few fishermen, fewer hunters, and no trappers; some birdwatchers come in for the glories of this songbird swamp, spectators like myself. The historical adventure of this place, I thought, ended when the *Emma K.* made her last run down the Canal, or when Holly made his steamwhistle sing "Nearer, My God, to Thee" that last time in the fields of Tadmore, or when Union Camp gave George Washington's Entry back to the American people, whence it came, and pulled out of these logwoods for good. Or maybe it really ended the last time Shelton Rountree spent a night camped on the Lake, the hair shivering and standing on the back of his neck at the bobcat's piercing nightcry, or the day the inveterate moonshiner Alvin Sawyer got busted for what must be good at his gargantuan still in the southern Dismal, or the morning Reggie Gregory walked from his kitchen out to his tractor shed staring as he trod the familiar fifty yards at the curtain of green to his left with deep and regretful certitude in his heart, knowing that even if he were offered the million dollars that Mose White made off the lost stand of juniper Reggie had carried him to, he could no longer find his own way back to the hollow cypress where yearly he had cached the traps whose steady catch pulled him through the Great Depression, and would never again oblige the rusting steel that lay awaiting his hand. Bear and deer will mark the spot, or some hiker lost and anxious will stumble inadvertently over the caved-in log and just as unpurposefully kick to flinders the rusty dust, logsplinters and all. Which moment, which event, marked the passing of the Swamp's adventure, who knew? Only the gods who made it, and they say little to the living of such things. I turned from the pink maple that shimmered in the breeze, and from the bethumping drums that had so well succeeded the rhythms of the rolling stock, walked south to my car at Five Points, and went down to the Lake for lunch.

Three weeks later, a few minutes past two on the hot Sunday

afternoon of May 18, 1986, a westbound Norfolk and Western steam engine pulling a company-picnic excursion train approached a switch called Juniper in the northern Swamp. One of the tracks in the heat of the day and under the pressure of the train became unsettled and shifted. The engineer—Robert Claytor, chairman and chief executive officer of Norfolk Southern and one of the most experienced steam engineers in America—felt a lateral motion as the locomotive passed over the turnout; a passenger in the first car behind the auxiliary water tender said the tender "rocked violently," and a passenger in the fourth car back reported "a jerk, side motion jerk, and to me it sounded like a loud explosion under the wheel . . . the sound of steel hitting steel." The trailing truck of the eighth car rode for some seven or eight yards up atop the steel ribbon, fell outside it, and then this and the next thirteen cars derailed, flipped, and jackknifed off to the rails' side and settled in the absolute Swamp as if they belonged there.

So much for the end of adventure in the Great Dismal, I thought when I heard of the trainwreck. Nothing is ever settled.

"The whole food counter started coming towards us," Navy Captain Robert Brewer told *The New York Times*. He and his two sons were in the dining car. "We realized we were going into the woods." There were a thousand men, women, and children aboard this rolling entertainment gone awry, and nearly two hundred of them were injured, mostly cuts and broken bones. The trainwreck was hard to get to, all the more so after two mobile cranes sent by the Navy in Norfolk to the site of the disaster got stuck in the stone driveway and blocked access from the east. Helicopters from the Coast Guard, the Navy, the State Police, all roared in, but only a small medevac copter—the "Nightingale"—could land at the scene of the derailment. Still, in three hours thirty emergency medical units evacuated these thousand people from the wreck in the Swamp. No one was killed, and no one later died of injuries, but, as Captain Kenneth Murphy of the Chesapeake Fire Department said, "There was some hollering."

And now the cries of the wounded that May day are ghost-cries on the winds that sough through the last juniper and cypress and whistle over the wilderness. And they join the desperate callings-out of Byrd's lost men on the 1728 survey line, and the mournful shanties and songs of Washington's rice-farmers and shingle-men, the shrieks and lamentations of French navymen with a payload of gold who by legend fled from a British man-of-war up the Southern Branch of Elizabeth River and into the Swamp where they hid their treasure and died at the hands of their pursuers, and the last rasping death-rattle breath of some outlaw slave with hellhounds on his trail, and with the name of Thomas Moore's death-cold maid that issuing from the lips of her lover wild and possessed rang on the Lake shore so long ago. This vast wild region is a place well fit for a grand gathering of ghosts, a place simultaneously aswarm with the spirits of all ages here, of fin, feather, fur, and manflesh; nor am I exempt.

I see myself on the Lake's north shore, at the mouth of Jericho and Washington, sitting one bright balmy October day with my little twins Hunter and Susannah, they just half a year old and already picking up the brown cypress needles from the ground and trying to devour them, and I at half my three score years and ten staring out at the rust-gold rim of Drummond in the fall. And I see two lovers one stormy April eve along the old Canal, my own sweet Ann Cary Kindell and I watching the quiet mists rise off the water and hang in the darkening pines. And at last I see in our Great Dismal Swamp not so much the indomitable sorrow it suggests as the incalculable and evolving beauty that it is.

Selected Swamp Sources

Drummond's Pond

The Great Dismal Swamp, edited by Paul W. Kirk, Jr. (Charlottesville: published for the Old Dominion University Research Foundation by the University Press of Virginia, 1979), is an excellent and invaluable collection, from which my work, particularly in its early chapters, has benefited greatly, drawing mainly on papers concerning geology and development of the Swamp; bola use; man's history here; remote sensing; forest dynamics and hydrology; and birds, mammals, and reptiles. For Governor Drummond's tale I am grateful to Thomas Jefferson Wertenbaker's *Virginia under the Stuarts* (New York: Russell and Russell, 1959) and *Torchbearer of the Revolution* (Princeton, N.J.: Princeton University Press, 1940), and to Stephen Beauregard Weeks's "William Drummond, First Governor of North Carolina" (*National Magazine* 15 [April 1892]: 616–28).

Juniper and *Washington's Entry*

For a clear understanding of early land acquisition, farming, and timbering pursuits, the direct and thorough "Man and the Great Dismal" (*Virginia Journal of Science* 27 [Fall 1976]: 141–71), by Edmund Berkeley and Dorothy Berkeley, is an essential historical text. So is Robert H. Reid's "History of the Dismal Swamp Land Company of Virginia" (Master's thesis, Duke University, 1948). Surveyor Jack Reid's short, unpublished "Report on Dismal Swamp" (Camp Manufacturing Company, 1952), tucked away in Union Camp's Swamp files in Franklin, Virginia, is a small, but real, treasure, a close-to-the-ground sketch of surveying and logging life in the Great Dismal. Another Union Camp document, helpful in its explication of title-chain intricacies in the northwest Swamp, is lawyer John C. Parker's "The Dismal Swamp: Memoranda Concerning Its History from 1763 to 1962" (Franklin, Va., October 1961).

Lost in the Desert

William Byrd's Histories of the Dividing Line betwixt Virginia and North Carolina, edited by William K. Boyd (Raleigh: North Carolina Historical Commission, 1929; reprint, with an introduction by Percy G. Adams [New York: Dover, 1967]), is a benchmark for Swamp surveyors of all stripes. C. R. Mason's "Mapping in Dismal Swamp" (*Military Engineer* 44 [March–April 1952]: 120–25), and the works of Berkeley and Berkeley, and of Jack Reid, bring the story of lines drawn in water and peat into the nineteenth and twentieth centuries. In *The North Carolina Gazetteer* (Chapel Hill: University of North Carolina Press, 1968), William S. Powell proposes 1715 as the possible year of first use of the name "dismal swamp" for this region. Robert C. McLean presents some of Samuel Perkins's diary as "A Yankee Tutor in the Old South" (*North Carolina Historical Review* 42 [January 1970]: 51–85). *Crusader in Crinoline* (Philadelphia: J. B. Lippincott, 1941) by Forrest Wilson includes an entertaining account of Harriet Beecher Stowe's writing *Dred*. Two fine surveys of Swamp works and lore are Robert Haywood Morrison's "The Literature and Legends of the Great Dismal Swamp" (Master's thesis, University of North Carolina at Chapel Hill, 1947) and the more recent "Essay on the Literature of the Dismal Swamp," by Peter C. Stewart, Paul W. Kirk, Jr., and Harold G. Marshall, in *The Great Dismal Swamp*. Porte Crayon's "The Dismal Swamp" (*Harper's New Monthly Magazine*, September 1856, 441–55) is a classic, and Alexander Hunter, in "The Great Dismal Swamp" (*Outing*, October 1895, 70–76) and *The Huntsman in the South* (New York and Washington: Neale, 1908), writes just as colorfully about the area.

At Large in the Swamp

Mrs. Ulrich Troubetzkoy's series "Seasons in the Dismal Swamp" (*Virginia Wildlife* 28[6] [Spring 1967]: 17–20; 28[8] [Summer 1967]: 4–5, 22–23; 28[10] [Fall 1967]: 6–8, 17; and 29[3] [Winter 1968]: 6–7, 12–22) captures life afield in the Swamp just prior to the Camp gift and creation of the National Wildlife Refuge, as does Jack Olsen's "The Cursed Swamp" (*Sports Illustrated*, November 26, 1962, 68–70, 72, 74–76, 79–82). And George W. Dean's "Forests and Forestry in the Dismal Swamp" (*Virginia Journal of Science* 20 [1969]: 166–73) offers valuable recollections about firefighting and anecdotes about Swamp liquormakers as well.

Canalbank Life

Alexander Crosby Brown's *The Dismal Swamp Canal* (Chesapeake, Va.: Norfolk County Historical Society of Chesapeake, 1970) and Berkeley and Berkeley's "Man and the Great Dismal" both cover the course of the Canal. More about early times in the area is in Wertenbaker's *Norfolk: Historic Southern Port* (Durham, N.C.: Duke University Press, 1931) and Jesse F. Pugh's and Frank T. Williams's *The Hotel in the Great Dismal Swamp* (Old Trap, N.C.: J. F. Pugh, 1964), and a short account on the "Reconstruction of the Dismal Swamp Canal" in *Scientific American*, March 5, 1898. Eleanor Cross and Charles Cross, Jr., edited *Glencoe Diary: The War-Time Journal of Elizabeth Curtis Wallace* (Chesapeake, Va.: Norfolk County Historical Society of Chesapeake, 1968), and journalist Charles Frederick Stansbury brought a lifetime of loving enthusiasm for the Swamp to his *The Lake of the Great Dismal* (New York: Albert and Charles Boni, 1925). From A. C. Brown and from W. J. Overman III's "James Adams Floating Theatre," *Pasquotank Historical Society Yearbook*, vol. 3 (Baltimore: Gateway Press, 1975), come stories of the old showboat.

Songbird Swamp

Brooke Meanley's observations on the Swamp's natural life and heritage are signal and include: "Natural History of the Swainson's Warbler" (U.S. Department of the Interior, North American Fauna, no. 69, Washington, D.C.: U.S. Government Printing Office, 1971), *Swamps, River Bottoms and Canebrakes* (Barre, Mass.: Barre Publishers, 1972), *The Great Dismal Swamp* (Washington, D.C.: Audubon Naturalist Society of the Central Atlantic States, 1973), and "An Analysis of the Birdlife of the Dismal Swamp" in the 1979 collection *The Great Dismal Swamp*. The surveyor's tale of impaled bears shows up in *Literary Digest*, March 14, 1931, 39–40. Paul Bartsch's 1901 *Osprey* piece, "A Trip to the Dismal Swamp," appears with a 1949 epilogue in *The Wood Thrush* 5 (1949–50): 12–20, and J. J. Murray's "The Great Dismal Swamp" in *The Raven* 19 (March–April 1948): 14–26, and are both worthy of naturalists' note.

The Great Dismal

The story of the great American poet's Swamp pilgrimage is drawn from *Robert Frost, a Biography* (New York: Holt, Rinehart and Winston, 1982) by Lawrance Thompson, that of Mahone's Confederate feint from Berkeley and Berkeley, and that of the excursion-train wreck from the National Transportation Safety Board's Railroad Accident Report (September 15, 1987) and *The New York Times* (May 19–21, 1986).

Illustration Credits

53   Photograph by Jack Reid, courtesy of the Virginia State Library and Archives, Richmond

55   Photograph by Surry Parker, courtesy of Elizabeth Parker Roberts

59   Photograph by Israel Cook Russell, courtesy of the US Geological Survey Photo Library, Denver, Colo.

74   Woodcut from an illustration by Porte Crayon, *Harper's New Monthly Magazine*, September 1856

75   Woodcut from an illustration by Porte Crayon, *Harper's New Monthly Magazine*, September 1856

77   Photograph by Israel Cook Russell, courtesy of the US Geological Survey Photo Library, Denver, Colo.

80   Woodcut from an illustration by Porte Crayon, *Harper's New Monthly Magazine*, September 1856

82   Photograph by Israel Cook Russell, courtesy of US Geological Survey Photo Library, Denver, Colo.

85   Photograph by Wirt A. Christian, Jr., courtesy of Virginia State Library and Archives, Richmond

87   Photograph by H. C. Mann, courtesy of Virginia State Library and Archives, Richmond

96   Photograph by Wirt A. Christian, Jr., courtesy of Virginia State Library and Archives, Richmond

108   Photograph by John Wallace II, courtesy of Elizabeth Parker Roberts

109   Photographer unknown, courtesy of North Carolina Collection, University of North Carolina, Chapel Hill

111   Photograph by Surry Parker, courtesy of Elizabeth Parker Roberts

113   Lithograph (1831) by Christopher Hall, from a drawing by Thomas Williamson, both of Norfolk, Va.

119   Photograph by Surry Parker, courtesy of Elizabeth Parker Roberts

120   Photograph by Surry Parker, courtesy of Elizabeth Parker Roberts

121   Photograph by Surry Parker, courtesy of Elizabeth Parker Roberts

124   Photograph by Surry Parker, courtesy of Elizabeth Parker Roberts

125   Photographer unknown, courtesy of Elizabeth Parker Roberts

127   Photograph by Israel Cook Russell, courtesy of US Geological Survey Photo Library, Denver, Colo.

130   Photograph by Israel Cook Russell, courtesy of US Geological Survey Photo Library, Denver, Colo.

139   Photograph by Brooke Meanley, used with his permission

146   Photograph by Brooke Meanley, used with his permission

152   Photograph by Israel Cook Russell, courtesy of US Geological Survey Photo Library, Denver, Colo.

154   Photograph courtesy of Weyerhauser, Tacoma, Wash.

163   Photograph by Brooke Meanley, used with his permission

165   Photograph by Brooke Meanley, used with his permission

Index